Yankees
SUCK!

Yankees SUCK!

The Unofficial Guide for Those Who Hate, Despise, Loathe, and Detest Those Bums from the Bronx

JIM GERARD

Roadside Amusements
Published by Chamberlain Bros.
a member of
Penguin Group (USA) Inc.
New York
2005

Roadside Amusements
Published by the Penguin Group
Penguin Group (USA) Inc., 375 Hudson Street, New York, New York 10014,
USA
Penguin Group (Canada), 10 Alcorn Avenue, Toronto, Ontario, Canada
M4V 3B2, (a division of Pearson Penguin Canada Inc.)
Penguin Books Ltd, 80 Strand, London WC2R 0RL, England
Penguin Ireland, 25 St Stephen's Green, Dublin 2, Ireland (a division of
Penguin Books Ltd)
Penguin Group (Australia), 250 Camberwell Road, Camberwell, Victoria
3124, Australia (a division of Pearson Australia Group Pty Ltd)
Penguin Books India Pvt Ltd, 11 Community Centre, Panchsheel Park,
New Delhi–110 017, India
Penguin Group (NZ), cnr Airborne and Rosedale Roads, Albany, Auckland
1310, New Zealand (a division of Pearson New Zealand Ltd)
Penguin Books (South Africa) (Pty) Ltd, 24 Sturdee Avenue, Rosebank,
Johannesburg 2196, South Africa

Penguin Books Ltd, Registered Offices: 80 Strand, London WC2R 0RL,
England

An application has been submitted to register this book with the
Library of Congress.

ISBN 1-59609-042-1

Printed in the United States of America
10 9 8 7 6 5 4 3 2 1

Book design by Jaime Putorti

Contents

Introduction

My friend Mike hates the Yankees. He hates them because in 1964, when he was 10 years old, they fired as manager his hero, Yogi Berra. When Yogi moved to the Mets for his career swan song, Mike went with him, and for the last 40 years, Mike has been a staunch Mets fan. But the ardor with which he supports his team pales in comparison to his loathing of the Yankees (which I believe has reached a cancerous stage). I honestly think he'd return the Mets' two championship trophies if that could somehow revoke all those Yankees flags.

All across the country, there are a lot of people like Mike—fans who have two favorite teams: their home team and whoever is playing against the Yankees that day.

Yankee Hating has become a cottage industry. Besides the ubiquitous YANKEES SUCK T-shirts, there's a "Discount Hate Yankees" channel on eBay, including a Hate Yankees Watch ($19.97), and Yankee Hater websites such as yankeessuck.com. (Who knows? Right now, someone out there may be hatching an anti-Yankee satellite radio station.)

This book is for all of you, from plumbers to professors, doctors to rockers—like the band Bender X, whose song "Yankees Suck," begins with a note to Yankees fans regarding Derek Jeter's efforts to remove equipment from Chuck Knoblauch's locker, specifically his balls.

We conceived of this as a handbook for Bomber bashers that shows how anyone, anywhere, of any age, can hate the Yankees like the most hardened denizen of Lansdowne Street in Boston. It's full of information, anecdotes, humor, and innuendo that will help you silence even the most truculent, arrogant Yankees fan, whether in a barroom argument or a bleacher donnybrook. Not least, it will help focus your rage, disappointment, and burning jealousy from opening day right up until the Yanks walk away with yet another completely undeserved World Series Championship.

Chapter One

SURE, THEY'RE SUCCESSFUL,
BUT THEY CHEAT

A s any Yankee fan will tell you within five seconds of meeting him, the Yankees are far and away the most successful team in the history of professional sports. This statement will usually be followed by a tally of their pennants and World Championships.

But the Yankee fan who gets in your face shouting "Thirty-nine!" or "Twenty-six!" like some demented bingo player won't ever explain how his beloved Bombers managed to haul in all that heavy gold leaf. Here's where you butt in and tell him the truth: that the Yankee glory is a whore, bought and paid for. Here are the real secrets to the Yankee success:

1. They patrol the free-agent waters like a great white shark, driving up prices and forcing other teams to the sidelines—and often, bidding against themselves. Which means the players and their agents love them. In the last few years alone, the Yanks have signed Mike Mussina, Jason Giambi, and Gary Sheffield (among others), plus re-upped home-grown stars such as Bernie Williams and Derek Jeter to long-term contracts equal to the gross national product of Togo. While these stars have contributed to Yankee pennants, these Faustian pacts come with a downside: All these players are aging and for the most part less productive. And they're unbenchable.

2. They lure stars who want to continue or finish their careers "playing on a winner" away from teams who know they can't afford to re-sign them as free agents. Take Exhibit A-Rod. Despite having the highest contract in baseball history—a cool $250 million over 10 years—the superstar agreed to forfeit his future as the greatest short-

stop in baseball history to play third base for the Yanks, who peddled a mercurial, rapidly aging (two years, overnight) talent in Alfonso Soriano to Texas. As if that wasn't bad enough, the Rangers agreed to pay a chunk of A-Rod's salary. (Later, it was rumored that Rangers owner Tom Hicks so wanted to divest himself of A-Rod's contract that he would've given him away for a YES network tote bag.) The fact that the Yanks have created their own market for talent is why you hear rumors that they're interested in almost every player in the big leagues. (What's next? YANKS REANIMATE LEFTY GROVE; WILL SURGICALLY ATTACH ARM TO FÉLIX HEREDIA'S BODY) At last season's trading deadline, the baseball world was shocked by the Yanks' failure to wrest Randy Johnson from Arizona, as if the D-backs had defied a papal decree. (The reason Johnson remained stranded in the desert was most likely Diamondbacks owner Jerry Colangelo's desire to avenge himself on Yankee owner George Steinbrenner for stealing David Wells out from under a handshake free-agent agreement two years earlier. See Chapter 11: Yankees Suck Across America.)

3. They pluck non-English-speaking international free agents blinded by the promise of big-city glamour and Jordanesque endorsement deals. Sometimes these sign-

ings are golden—Hideki Matsui, Orlando "El Duque" Hernández—while others are the baseball equivalent of back-alley abortions, botchings that the team tries to bury as quickly as possible. Think of Hideki Irabu, who went from golden-armed prospect to "fat pussy toad"— what Steinbrenner called the pitcher after an exhibition game when he forgot that his job description included occasionally covering first base—and Andy Morales, a Cuban third baseman who couldn't excel even in the Eastern League and who clambered around the hot corner like a dancing bear that had escaped from the Russian circus. (The Yanks so soured on Morales that they tried to back out of his contract by claiming that he had misrepresented his age, which proves that lying about your birth date is only acceptable if, like El Duque and Soriano, you produce.)

4. They fill out the back of their roster with substitute outfielders and set-up men (e.g., Steve Karsay and Tom Gordon) who would be stars on other clubs but who—like matinee idols who work for a pittance just to be in a Woody Allen picture—are willing to become glorified spear-carriers for YankeeBucks. (This gives me an idea: The team could print its own money, which would be standard

currency only among baseball players and their agents. The colorful higher-denomination bills would feature Yankee greats—Joe DiMaggio on the thousand, Mickey Mantle on the hundred, and so on, with Stump Merrill on the face of the penny.)

The Yankees can do all this—gobbling up one prized asset after another like a corporate raider—because they have unique competitive advantages:

✦ Geography. They play in the largest metropolitan region in the country, home to more than 20 million people. They share it with only one other major league team—the poorly run Mets—when by all accounts it has the population to support five clubs. Steinbrenner bought the Yankees from CBS in 1972 for $10 million—about $3 million less than CBS had originally paid! The franchise is now estimated to be worth $832 million. Darren Rovell, the sports business reporter for ESPN.com, says, "What [Steinbrenner] was buying was not just the team, but the rights to the New York market, the biggest in the country, with all its revenue streams."[1]

✦ Attendance. The Yankees led the American League in home and road attendance last year, drawing close to 4 million fans in 2004, their all-time record at the Stadium. *Forbes* magazine stated that they made $119 million in gate receipts in 2003 as part of their total revenues of $238 million. That means they could close the Stadium to fans and, based on media and marketing income, have a $119 million payroll, which would still be the largest in baseball. In New York, the team has become a cultural institution, like MoMA and *The Producers*, declared general manager Brian Cashman to the *New York Times*. So now people come to Yankee games not to steal a souvenir ball from an innocent child or vomit on their neighbors but *to be seen* doing same. The Yankees have been perennially first in road attendance, even during the team's mid-'60s descent. After all, the Yankees are loathed by fans everywhere (See Chapter 11: Yankees Suck Across America), and even the lowliest Royals fan eagerly heads to the park when the Yanks come to town, knowing that if his club can trounce the lordly Bombers, the season won't be a total loss.

✦ Cable money. Although the Yankees are demonized for exploiting their superior economic advantages, their financial domination didn't really start until 1988 when, amid an explosive growth in cable television, the Madison Square Garden network paid $486 million over 12 years for the rights to telecast the team's games. Neil DeMause, author of *Field of Schemes*, a study of the ways in which professional sports franchises extort new stadiums from cities, says that "When it comes to creative accounting, the Boss has always been at the cutting edge."[2] In the 1980s, Steinbrenner paid himself a "consulting fee" to negotiate his own cable contract. In 2002, after the team failed to come to an agreement with Cablevision's MSG network to telecast their games, Steinbrenner realized that owning his own cable network was a much better deal. It offered potential riches, greater control over what its announcers said, and a way to market his games, tickets, players, and merchandise 365 days a year. So the Yanks partnered with Goldman Sachs, the New Jersey Nets, and the New Jersey Devils to set up YES, for Yankees

Entertainment and Sports (assuming you consider Michael Kay's celebrity anilingus, otherwise known as "Center Stage," entertaining). Goldman Sachs and Providence Equity invested $340 million for their 40 percent share; Yankee Global Enterprises owns 35 percent; and some former Nets and current Devils owners own the rest. No one knows exactly how much revenue the Yankees derive from YES—neither the Yankees nor YES are obligated to open their books to the public—but estimates range from $50 million to $100 million. Like other clubs who are part of media companies, the team shuffles YES revenue to the baseball side of the accounting ledger, where it remains protected from MLB's revenue-sharing agreement. DeMause says, "George is taking fifty million dollars out of one of his pockets and putting it in another . . . helping him evade attempts by fellow owners to force him to share the bounty that comes from operating the most lucrative franchise in baseball." Bud Selig has made noises about auditing the Yankees, but for now the Yanks continue to save as much as $20 million a year with this sleight of hand. (Of course, once they had leveraged their deal with the Devils, the Yanks broke up the cartel.) Another way the Yanks subvert the revenue-sharing agreement is to shift some of their merchandising efforts to the YES network website. The Yanks could potentially rake in another $10 million or so if they sold the naming rights to their stadium, either the current one or the proposed new one they're trying to shake down from the city. (See Chapter 6: Condemning the House That Ruth Built.) For example, the Yanks might potentially be able to sell the naming rights to the multinational of their choice. ("It's Zoloft Night at Pfizer Park. All depressives get half-price admission, plus a Dr. Phil bobblehead.") However, either because their lease with New York City prevents it or they felt they would lose "brand" equity, the team has decided against it. Instead, they did the next best thing . . .

✦ All major league baseball clubs are party to a marketing agreement, which mandates that they equally share the profits from the sale of merchandise, use of team logos, etc. In 1999, Steinbrenner signed an independent, 10-year, $94 million sponsorship deal with Adidas—money that the other clubs couldn't touch.

When commissioner Bud Selig nixed the deal, George sued, claiming that the other owners were acting as a cartel unfairly restraining trade. Selig caved, and the deal went ahead. In 2001, the team made cross-promotional deals with Manchester United, the Yankees of England's Premier League soccer, giving YES the right to telecast Man U's games in America. Another move that yields a few million a year was selling special Japanese advertising signage to display behind home plate during games—ads targeted not just at New York's Japanese community, but at the millions of fans back in Japan who worship Hideki Matsui like he's the emperor and now get to watch 135 big-league games a year thanks to a six-year, $200 million rights deal that Major League Baseball signed with Dentsu in 2003. (Eighty percent of those games involve the Yankees, Mets, or Mariners.)

◆ When you combine the huge fan pool and windfall media deals that arise from perfect location, plus Enronesque bookkeeping feats, you end up with the biggest advantage of all:

◆ Payroll.

These are the major league team payrolls as of mid-2004:[3]

1. New York Yankees $183,335,513
2. Boston $125,208,542
3. Anaheim $101,909,667
4. New York Mets $95,754,304
5. Philadelphia $93,219,167
6. Chicago Cubs $91,101,667
7. Los Angeles $89,694,343
8. Atlanta $88,507,788
9. San Francisco $82,019,166
10. St. Louis $81,008,517
11. Seattle $78,483,834
12. Houston $74,666,303
13. Arizona $70,204,984
14. Colorado $68,610,403
15. Chicago White Sox $68,262,500
16. San Diego $63,689,503
17. Oakland $59,825,167
18. Texas $59,025,973
19. Minnesota $53,585,000

20. Toronto $50,017,000

21. Detroit $49,828,554

22. Baltimore $49,212,653

23. Kansas City $47,609,000

24. Montreal $43,197,500

25. Cincinnati $42,722,858

26. Florida $42,118,042

27. Pittsburgh $40,227,929

28. Cleveland $34,569,300

29. Tampa Bay $28,706,667

30. Milwaukee $27,518,500

The Yanks top the list, as they have for most of the last decade. A brief glance at the payroll disparity between New York and the clubs on the bottom of the list means they pay their starting rotation as much as some clubs' entire payrolls. It also means that the Yankees could buy the entire rosters of Montreal/Washington, Cincinnati, Pittsburgh, Tampa Bay, and Milwaukee, with enough left over to sign a couple of defecting "imperialist lackeys" from Cuba. They could make those teams play their own five-team fantasy league—in the nude. Or move the Pirates to, say, Vladivostok. On the other hand, George might pay back Bud Selig for levying the luxury tax on him by turning Miller Field into a used-car lot.

But why bother shopping at Wal-Mart when you can afford Tiffany's? The Yanks much prefer to spend their $183 million or so on superstars, who they pay like gods, and middle relievers, who they pay like superstars. Here are the available figures for the current Yankee payroll, broken down by player:[4]

Alex Rodriguez	$21,726,881
Derek Jeter	$18,600,000
Mike Mussina	$16,000,000
Kevin Brown	$15,714,286
Jason Giambi	$12,428,571
Bernie Williams	$12,357,143
Gary Sheffield	$12,029,131
Mariano Rivera	$10,890,000
Jorge Posada	$9,000,000
Javier Vásquez	$9,000,000
John Olerud	$7,700,000
Hideki Matsui	$7,000,000
Steve Karsay	$6,000,000
Esteban Loaiza	$4,000,000

Tom Gordon	$3,500,000
Paul Quantrill	$3,000,000
Kenny Lofton	$2,985,551
Jon Lieber	$2,700,000
Travis Lee	$2,000,000
Félix Heredia	$1,800,000
Rubén Sierra	$1,000,000
Miguel Cairo	$900,000
John Flaherty	$775,000
Tony Clark	$750,000
Enrique Wilson	$700,000
Orlando Hernández	$500,000
Donovan Osborne	$450,000
C. J. Nitkowski	$350,000
Jorge DePaula	$302,550
Bubba Crosby	$301,400

OK, let's break this down:

✦ A-Rod's contract is huge, but thanks to the kind of perverse socialism that only exists among owners of professional sports franchises, his former employer, Tom Hicks, is paying a hefty chunk.

- They paid Kevin Brown about $3 million to punch a clubhouse wall (after being spanked by the Sox during the regular season, Brown broke his non-pitching hand taking his frustrations out on a wall that was clearly asking for trouble), and another five or six million went to the intestinal parasite that sidelined the psychotic pitcher for over a month. (If you factor in the parasite that crippled Giambi for several months . . . sorry, Enrique Wilson, they paid a microorganism about ten times what you made. Of course, the parasite had a much better year.)

- Mussina missed almost two months—which comes to a loss of around $5.5 million—and even at his best, he's always been not quite good enough to win post-season contests or Cy Young Awards, or to pitch perfect games. (Even his best friend calls him "Mr. Almost.")

- Bernie Williams seems to have popped a few strings and is ready to enter his next stage of life—guitarist wannabe who is patronized by real musicians for his jock-celebrity value.

- What can you say about Gary Sheffield, who's either a transparent liar or so dumb that, as he claims, he thought the steroid "cream" he was sold by a juice-peddling member of Barry Bonds's entourage at the now-infamous BALCO lab was some sort of high-octane Tiger Balm. While Sheff had a great year, the possibility of his indictment by John Ashcroft and subsequent disciplinary action from Major League Baseball could cause the team big problems, especially if it happens after free-agent hunting season. Future: Joins uncle Dwight Gooden in special Detox Wing of the Hall of Fame.

✦ Mariano Rivera, while still great, is no longer Superman. While God may have been guiding his arm in the past, the Lord now looks like he's putting his smart money behind guys like Brad Lidge and Francisco Rodriguez. Off-season plans: Visit to snake-handling faith healer to restore velocity on cut fastball. Result: Faith healer more effective than Mel Stottlemyre.

✦ Jorge Posada. Each passed ball is worth, let's say, $200,000. Starting to approach age when catchers fall apart like IKEA furniture.

✦ Javier Vásquez. A $9-million bust with worse mechanics than the Edsel. Excuse: Not used to pitching in public. Rumor is that some of the Yankee brain trust wants to relocate him.

- José Contreras. The Yanks thought that back-channel negotiations to release his family (they threatened to jam Cuban airwaves with replays of John Sterling's "The-uh-uh Yankees win!") would straighten out the enigmatic Contreras, but familiarity breeds an ERA of 6. Nicknamed by Fidel Castro "El Titan de Bronze," he crumpled like aluminum foil when facing a bunch of Boston "cowboys" with ugly goatees. Yanks saved $12 million by blasting "the Cuban Missile" to Chicago for . . .

- Esteban Loaiza. The Yanks anted up approximately $2 million for two months' work. He was hit so hard that he needed a Kevlar uniform, and he left the Yankee Stadium pitchers' mound in such bad shape, Jeb Bush was seen touring it.

- John Olerud. More stationary than the Washington Monument and plays with just as much emotion. Rumor is he made his last 100 plate appearances while dead. Well, he only cost them the waiver price of $25,000, which is about right for a guy who, like an overprotected child, still wears his batting helmet in the field.

- Six million for Steve Karsay, who spent most of the

last two years trying to recover from a torn labrum. He was said to have "left five miles per hour on the operating table" (promptly filched by El Duque), and returned to toss a few ceremonial innings in meaningless September games in preparation for next year's Old-Timers Day.

✦ You could call Travis Lee a "million-dollar hitter," because that's how much the Yankees paid him for each of the two hits he notched (in 19 at-bats) before injuring his shoulder and missing almost the entire season.

What's most astonishing about the Yanks' profligate 2004 payroll is that for $184 million, they fielded a below-average pitching staff, middle relief worthy of Freddy Krueger, and a bench that's baseball's version of *Cocoon*. Teams like the Pirates can cobble together a 1–6 bullpen off the scrap heap of failed prospects, Rule V claimants, and minor-league free agents, but the Yankees—as if trying to channel the 1969 alumni squad—can do no better than Donovan Osborn, Bret Prinz, and Tanyon Sturtze.

Yanks Lead
Big-League Paymasters

The Yanks led the majors in payroll, as they have for most of the last 20 years, as the following list demonstrates:

1985: $15.40M (1st in majors)

1986: $17.25M (1st in majors)

1987: $18.57M (1st in majors)

1988: $21.52M (1st in majors)

1989: $18.48M (4th in majors)

1990: $20.59M (7th in majors)

1991: $31.94M (7th in majors)

1992: $34.90M (8th in majors)

1993: $46.59M (3rd in majors)

1994: $47.51M (1st in majors)

1995: $58.17M (1st in majors)

1996: $61.51M (1st in majors)

1997: $73.39M (1st in majors)

1998: $73.96M (2nd in majors)

1999: $91.99M (1st in majors)

2000: $113.37M (1st in majors)

2001: $109.79M (1st in majors)*

2002: $125.93M (1st in majors)*

2003: $164M (1st in majors)*

*Opening Day payrolls; all others are September 1 totals.

Source: The late Doug Pappas's Business of Baseball pages

NOTES

1. Interview with the author, October 12, 2004.

2. Interview with the author, October 7, 2004.

3. Darren Rovell, interview, October 12, 2004.

4. All payroll figures taken from ESPN.com.

Chapter Two

ALL-TIME WORST
YANKEE TRADES

We all know about the Curse of the Bambino and all of the other magical acquisitions that boosted the team's fortunes. However, the Bombers have made their share of personnel blunders. And while most of the really egregious deals were engineered by Bad George, the team has a history of transactional boners, starting even before they worked their Ruthian mojo on the Red Sox. Here are the all-time worst Yankee moves:

1. Yanks put pitcher Hippo Vaughn on waivers, 1912.[1] Technically not a trade, but a blundering move that cost the team roughly 150 wins. In 1910, Jim "Hippo" Vaughn, a flame-throwing young southpaw, was recalled from the minors by the New York Americans (the team's official name right before it was changed to the Yankees in 1913, thus making its players baseball's version of the Quarrymen). As writer Steven Goldman of *Baseball Prospectus* tells it, Vaughn, who acquired his nickname as much for his lumbering running style as his girth, won 13 games with a 1.83 ERA. He got off to a slow start the following year, and when manager Harry Wolverton demoted him to Providence of the International League, Vaughn—in a display of independence rare for players of that plantation era—refused to report unless he was given a stipend. New York waived him. Manager Clark Griffith of the Washington Senators thought Vaughn still had his stuff and plucked him off the waiver wire. Although Vaughn went on to pair with Walter Johnson and boost the Senators' fortunes, a couple of years later, Griffith, too, let him go. He went on to become the greatest left-handed pitcher in Chicago Cubs history, going 124–77 from 1914 to 1919, starting a World Series game (against Babe Ruth of the Red

Sox), and dueling Reds pitcher Fred Toney in a nine-inning double no-hitter in 1917.

2. Yanks trade pitcher Stan Bahnsen to the Chicago White Sox for third baseman Rich McKinney, 1971. Bahnsen won 21 games for the White Sox in 1972, while McKinney failed to win the Yankees' third-base job (he was beaten out by Mexican League refugee Celerino Sanchez). He hit .215 in 37 games, and he tied an AL record with four errors at third in one game. Over his short career—341 games—McKinney hit .225 with 20 homers and 100 RBI. Bahnsen pitched another nine years and finished his career with a 146–149 record and a 3.61 ERA, pitching mostly for weak teams.

In 1972, the Yanks had a rotation of Mel Stottlemyre, the Swapmeet Twins Mike Kekich and Fritz Peterson, Steve Kline, and Rob Gardner. They finished 79–76, in fourth place, 6½ games behind Detroit. Richard Lally, author of *Bombers*, an oral history of the Yankees, calls Bahnsen-for-McKinney "a deal that probably cost the Yanks the 1972 Eastern Division title."[2]

3. Yanks trade outfielder/DH Oscar Gamble and minor-league pitchers LaMarr Hoyt and Bob Polinsky plus approximately $200,000 to the Chicago White Sox for shortstop Bucky Dent, 1977. Let's face it: George's Yankees eat their young. Hoyt, a farmhand at the time of the trade, was no exception.

He was buried in the minors at the time of the trade, but within two years—as soon as he joined the Chicago rotation in 1982—he excelled. He won his first nine decisions to tie a White Sox record and finished 19–15, leading the league in wins and walking only 48 batters in 239.2 innings. He was even better in 1983. He won 24 games, going 15–2 after the All-Star break, led the White Sox to the AL West title, and won the Cy Young award in a landslide. Hoyt walked just 31 batters that year, just three more than Cy Young's record low of 28 in 1904. In the ALCS opener against Baltimore, he tossed a five-hitter for Chicago's only win.

As if to stick it to his former team, in 1985 Hoyt fired a one-hitter against the Yankees in Comiskey Park, allowing only a scratch single to Don Mattingly. So what if he later developed a drug problem, was suspended from baseball for a year, and went to prison twice? He would've made an ideal member of the late '80s "rap sheet" Yanks.

Gamble, who the Yanks had obtained in late 1975 for pitcher Pat Dobson in December 1975, hit 17 homers and knocked in 57 runs in only 340 at-bats to help boost the team to its first pennant in 12 years. But the slugging right-fielder had a personal issue that the buttoned-down organization couldn't countenance: an Afro that resembled a mutant Chia pet (after all, it was the Superfly era). The 'fro added more than four inches to his height, sometimes popped his batting helmet off, and, for all we know, may have lengthened his strike zone.

It sure didn't affect his hitting: In 1978 with Chicago, Gamble had his best season: He hit .297 with career highs of 31 homers, 83 RBIs, 75 runs scored, and 22 doubles in only 408 at-bats, and the White Sox contended, improving to 90–72 from 64–97. The Yanks eventually realized their mistake and reacquired him in August 1979 in a deal that also sent Mickey Rivers to the Rangers.

As for Dent, he acquired the middle name "Fuckin'" from Red Sox fans after his 1978 playoff homer. And although he is revered in Yankeeland, the man he replaced at shortstop, Fred Stanley, was just as good defensively and would have at least equaled, if not surpassed, Dent's run production: Their OPS (on-base-plus-slugging) averages are nearly identical, even though Stanley only played part-time (he may have improved as a regular).

In summation, the Yankees traded a guy who hit more than 30 homers the following season plus a future Cy Young Award winner for a player they didn't need. In Lally's analysis, "Hoyt was not a great pitcher; he really didn't deserve that Cy Young. But he was solid, and in his last good season went 16–8 for the 1985 Padres. If the Yanks had him that year, they'd have won another division title."[3]

4. In a move that went virtually unnoticed, the Yanks trade 22-year-old outfield prospect and future MVP Willie McGee to the St. Louis Cardinals for sore-armed lefty Bob Sykes, 1981. The Bombers felt that they had an outfield surplus and could afford to deal the switch-hitting McGee. The next year, the Cards called up McGee, who batted .296 while swiping 24 bases and coming in third in Rookie of the Year voting, as the Cardinals defeated the Milwaukee Brewers in the World Series. McGee had supersonic legs—Cardinals manager Whitey Herzog said that he was the fastest runner he'd ever seen, even faster than Mickey Mantle—a great ability to make contact, and all-encompassing range (he won three Gold Gloves). The slap-hitting McGee joined Vince Coleman and Ozzie Smith as a major catalyst for the jackrabbit Cardinal teams of the

'80s, who would win two more pennants after 1982. McGee won the batting title in 1985 with a .353 average, the highest in history for a switch-hitter, while stealing 56 bases and scoring 114 runs. In 1987, he banged home 105 runs. In 1990, McGee won his second National League batting title despite playing the last six weeks of the season for Oakland. He retired in 1999 with a lifetime .295 average.

As for Sykes? He was a below-average part-time starter and long reliever even while healthy, but after the Yanks acquired him, the arm problems that had plagued him throughout his five-year career grew worse. He never pitched an inning for the Yanks, or for any other major-league team. After one season in the minors, it was bye-bye baseball, hello Aflac. Showing either a rare degree of magnanimity or a desperate need for vicarious fame, Sykes later said, "Personally, and I mean this from the bottom of my heart, it will be an honor for the rest of my life to be known in baseball as the player traded for Willie McGee."

What was ironic about the deal was that at the precise moment he traded the swift-footed McGee, Steinbrenner had decided that he wanted to construct a speed-oriented,

National League–style team. But instead of keeping the speedster who could actually play, they let him go and signed no-talents such as free agent Dave Collins, who could run everywhere but to first base.

Clearly, George has a luxury box on the karmic wheel. Before the 2004 season, he overruled his baseball people and signed an over-the-hill Kenny Lofton, who possessed little of his original speed or anything else. It was a case of TWI—Trading While Intoxicated, in this case by the Marlin's Juan Pierre and his disruption of the Yanks' defense in the 2003 Series. Look for animatronic George to sign a one-legged José Reyes around 2116.

5. In a six-degrees-of-Yankee-separation linkage, Collins, pitcher Mike Morgan, and minor leaguer Fred McGriff are packed off to the Blue Jays for pitcher Dale Murray and minor leaguer Tom Dodd, in late 1982. This trade in a nutshell: The Yanks gave away 493 home runs and a borderline Hall of Famer for about 120 innings of sub-par relief.

6. In yet another stupid trade of prospects for aging veterans, the Yankees deal pitchers Brian Fisher, Doug Drabek, and Logan Easley to the Pirates for pitchers Rick Rhoden, Cecilio Guante, and Pat Clements, in 1986. The right-handed Drabek had a decent rookie season in 1985,

after which the Yanks decided to continue the baseball version of Live Aid, dispatching him to the rebuilding Pirates. Under pitching coach Ray Miller, Drabek expanded his repertoire from a fastball and a slider to include a changeup and a lethal curveball. After combining for 29 wins the next two years, Drabek went 22–6 with a 2.76 ERA to win the NL Cy Young award in 1990. He pitched brilliantly—although with tough luck—in Pittsburgh's three straight playoff appearances from 1991 to 1993, and over his six years with the Pirates he went 92–62.

Meanwhile, the Bucs must've rolled back the odometer on the reliable Rhoden's arm, for after a solid first season in New York, during which he went 16–10, he had only 1½ years of mediocre ball left.

The Drabek deal also illuminates another weakness of the reign of King George: a chronic inability to develop pitchers. There was Ron Guidry in the 1970s, Dave Righetti in the 1980s, and Andy Pettitte and Mariano Rivera in the 1990s. That's it: four pitchers in 30 years. This is in spite— or because—of a merry-go-round of pitching coaches, the sole prerequisite for which seemed to be a last name of Connors. They've drafted busts (including Brian Taylor, a #1 overall draft choice who, before he could even join the

Yanks' system, destroyed his shoulder—and his career—in a barroom fight), traded promising prospects, and have been completely unable to coax kinetic performances out of potential talent. An increasing amount of criticism is finding current pitching coach Mel Stottlemyre, who first burned out brilliant talents Dwight Gooden, Ron Darling, and Sid Fernández while with the 1980s Mets. Not only has Stott been unable to shape what little young talent comes through the pipeline, but top-of-the-line pitchers such as Javier Vásquez seem to lose their effectiveness under his watch. Call him the anti–Leo Mazzone.

7. Yanks trade Jay Buhner and two minor-league nonentities to the Seattle Mariners for Ken Phelps, mid-season, 1988, in the only baseball trade ever immortalized on a sitcom. In an episode of *Seinfeld,* Larry David's Steinbrenner tells Frank Costanza—played by Jerry Stiller—that his son is missing and presumed dead.

COSTANZA: What in the hell did you trade Jay Buhner for? He had thirty home runs, over a hundred RBIs last year. He's got a rocket for an arm. You don't know what the hell you're doin'!

STEINBRENNER: Well, Buhner was a good prospect, no question about it. But my baseball people love Ken

Phelps's bat. They kept saying "Ken Phelps, Ken Phelps, Ken Phelps."

The Yanks acquired a 34-year-old DH (who admittedly was having a good year) in exchange for a 24-year-old outfielder with Paul Bunyanesque power and a rocket arm, who they were convinced—after only 81 big-league at-bats—had holes in his swing the size of the Grand Canyon. George told manager Lou Piniella that Phelps would seal the pennant for the Yankees, who were sitting atop a tight Eastern Division field. Inevitably, Phelps hit .224 with only 17 home runs in 122 games for the Yankees before being dealt to Oakland the next year. The Bombers, meanwhile, finished fifth.

Within three years, Buhner had become Seattle's right fielder, belting 27 homers, while Phelps was out of baseball and en route to the Old DH Home. As Jay Jaffe assessed it on his blog, Futility Infielder, "In trading for a ballplayer past his already-squandered prime, they passed up a chance at the next Ken Phelps, the kind of player you really don't need to give up anything of significance to acquire." The Yanks of that era operated like a mass exporter of home runs (see Fred McGriff): Over his 15-year career, Buhner hit 310 home runs and slugged .494 with a .359 on-base average. His home-run percentage of 6.18 per 100 at-bats places him 22nd all-time. He hit 20 home runs or more for seven straight years, including the string of three 40+ seasons from 1995 to 1997. He hit a key home run in Game 2 of the 2000 ALDS against the White Sox, and his final blast—a valedictory "Fuck you" to the organization that had banished him—came in the 2001 ALCS against the Yankees.

In addition to his on-field value, "Bone" Buhner also served as a Veeckian promotional tool for the M's. In honor of their balding right-fielder ("the style is hereditary," Buhner explained) the club sponsored the first "Jay Buhner Haircut Night" in 1994. Four hundred and twenty-six "Twisted Buhner Fans"—including two women—got free admission for agreeing to have their heads shaved. This later became an annual event, renamed "Buhner Buzz-Cut Night," in which thousands of fans sacrificed their hair, some wearing T-shirts emblazoned with the slogan AMERICA THE BUHNERFUL.[4]

The Buhner-for-Phelps deal not only hurt the Yanks in the long term; it was also a poor short-term option. According to Lally, "They could have gotten Mike Boddicker for Buhner in 1988, which might have brought them another division title."

NOTES

1. Steven Goldman, Baseball Prospectus, 2004.

2. Interview with the author, September 2004.

3. Ibid.

4. From www.baseballlibrary.com.

Chapter Three

THE FANS

You die and go to Hell, these things happen. You're expecting fire, brimstone, banishment from God's presence. But instead of Satan—or worse, some Ivy League intern—you're confronted by a drunken lout missing several teeth who has an Anglo-Saxonism tattooed on the inside of his lower lip. He's completely naked, except for a blue cloth cap sporting the interlocking "NY." He greets you with the words, "You suck!"

Then you realize that your punishment is even worse

than you anticipated, and that you've mistakenly fallen into the ninth circle of Hell, the one reserved for Yankee fans. And that you will spend the rest of eternity being reminded of all the World Championships, taunted, punched out, and besoddened with stale beer, while being forced to watch it all broadcast on the biggest Jumbotron you've ever seen.

As Gay Talese wrote almost 50 years ago, "There are fans—and there are Yankee fans." They're a mutant species, all right. Spoiled, vulgar front-runners who sprout like fungi when the team clinches another pennant, only to slither back under their rocks at the first sign of a losing streak. Insecure losers who try to live vicariously through a bunch of multimillionaires. Neanderthals who, when they stop brawling with the opposition fans, turn their inchoate rage on each other. Storm troopers of couchpotatodom in JETER T-shirts who strut through the baseball universe with a bellicose sense of entitlement, then wonder, "Why do they hate us?" Feral creatures who turn the bleachers into their own jungle preserve and have been known to dangle their victims over the facing of the upper deck.

They've been called "the ugly Americans of sport who

flaunt an assumption of wealth and dominance"[1] and "the closest thing this country has to soccer hooligans."[2]

And since the team started winning again in the mid-1990s, they've spread like algae: The smarmy guy in accounting who wears a Yankee T-shirt with his designer-knockoff suit. The loutish brother-in-law who interrupts grace at Thanksgiving dinner to bellow about Jeter's "clutch"-ness. The drunken miscreants who used to take every opportunity to taunt Red Sox fans with the chant "1918!"—Boston's last championship before 2004 being the only fact they know about that year ("World War One? Who gives a shit?") and possibly the only historical detail of any kind that's rattling around the empty warehouses of their brains. The pathetic, whiny, live-with-their-mother shut-ins who have a less active social life than Norman Bates and pester sports-talk jocks with their embarrassing tantrums and delusional trade proposals: "Mad Dog, WE GOTTA TRADE BRAD HALSEY AND FELIX ESCALONA FOR THE BIG UNIT! IT'S A NO-BRAINER!" The pandering politicos like carpetbagger Hillary Clinton, whose lead-footed attempt to ingratiate herself with New Yorkers during her senatorial campaign by wearing a Yankee cap was met with derision, even by Yankee fans. If she were a home-run ball, they would have thrown her back.

Taken individually, Yankee fans are a bad day at the beach, but a stadium full of them is exponentially scarier and amplifies the team's fascistic overtones—its kitschy mythologizing, perpetual usurping of other teams' players, and cheerleading by Mussolini-in-training Rudy Giuliani. In Bob Woodward's *Bush at War*, Karl Rove is even quoted comparing the reaction of a New York Yankee crowd to an appearance by Bush as being "like a Nazi rally." And—let's face it—they're owned by an evil genius who would love nothing more than to clone a master race of free agents.

With all their pennants and championships, you'd think Yankee fans would be euphoric. But instead, they're a miserable lot who seem unable to derive any satisfaction from their team's success. For them, winning is like crack—no amount is ever enough and they can't live without it. That's what leads to their strange junkie-like behavior, which Yankee fan-blogger Larry Mahnken calls "arrogant paranoia." Mahnken posted on his Replacement Level Yankee Blog, "[Yankee fans] lack any confidence in the starting pitching, the relief pitching, and even the lineup, but then they express absolute certainty that they'll win the World Series anyway, not because of their strength, but because the Red Sox and Cardinals will 'choke.'"

That's dementia, all right. But then again, we're talking about Yankee fans, the best of whom are tortured sociopaths and the worst of whom are ...

BLEACHER CREATURES

The Yankee image is bland, upper-class, corporate. Always has been. You see this in the demeanor of the players, who approach the game with the assiduousness of grim bureaucrats (what sportswriters call "professionalism"). You also see it in the core of their fan base—baronial types hermetically ensconced in their luxury boxes and upper-middle-class frat-man execs from Westchester. Talese nailed Yankee fandom almost 50 years ago: "Wall Street bankers back the Yankees; Smith College girls approve of them. God, Brooks Brothers, and United States Steel are believed to be solidly in the Yankees' corner."[3] So no, the Bombers aren't exactly the people's team ...

... except for one corner of Yankee Stadium, 2,385 seats spread over 27 rows of backless benches in Section 39, inhabited by wild denizens whose booing, boozing, and brawling has turned the area into the Outhouse That Ruth Built.

They call themselves the Bleacher Creatures, and they're loud, violent, abusive, ADDled troglodytes. They have to be herded into Yankee Stadium through two back entrances (they're not allowed anywhere else) and are under surveillance by two New York City cops and two stadium security guards. They spend the entire game clapping, chanting, cursing, banging on percussion instruments, and dissing everything that moves—the opposing right-fielder, slumping Yankees, the umps, the program vendor, box-seat holders, fans with colorfully dyed hair ("East Village! East Village!"), and Dick Cheney, who they booed when he attended a Yankees game and his picture was flashed on the scoreboard (proving they recognize a fellow asshole when they see one). They even learned Japanese obscenities to greet Ichiro Suzuki when he made his first New York appearance. They were the only baseball fans to boo and insult Blue Jays first baseman Carlos Delgado for refusing to stand during the playing of *God Bless America* to protest against the U.S. war in Iraq.

In 1985, they even jeered vocalist Mary O'Dowd so vociferously while she sang the Canadian national anthem that she stopped in midsong and ran off the field crying.[4] And of course, they have a long Yankee tradition of booing their own hometown heroes, including Joe DiMaggio and Roger Maris, who they abused so mercilessly during his 1961 chase of Babe Ruth's home-run record that it caused the sensitive right-fielder's hair to fall out. (Remember what Bob Uecker once said of Philadelphia fans—"They'd boo Santa Claus"? Well, Bleacher Creatures wouldn't only boo St. Nick, they'd kick the crap out of him and his elves, too. "That's for not bringing us a lefty specialist last December!")

The Creatures are a fraternity of sadists who exploit the personal shortcomings of Yankee opponents. (They seem to have advance scouts.) They so cruelly heckled Chicago White Sox outfielder Wil Cordero—who had pled guilty to spousal battery in the off-season—that, after he'd played the first game of a three-game series in right field, the team moved him to another position (out of earshot) for the next two games. And their taunts to David Justice of "Hal-le Ber-ry!" (Justice's ex-wife, who accused him of domestic violence) are celebrated among connoisseurs of malicious mockery. The Creatures make no bones about their mean-spiritedness. One admitted to Dan Raley of the Seattle *Post-Intelligencer*, "The best part is when we find out the intimate details. You know, something that goes on in their life, like drugs, or booze, marital problems, or wife-beating. What we do to these guys, if people did that to me at my job every day, I'd shoot myself."

Just in case the targeted opposing players don't get the verbal message, the Creatures indiscriminately hurl whatever objects are at hand. Sticks, stones, coins, knives, batteries, inflatable dolls, transistor radios, heads of cabbage (the last three items were all hurled at José Canseco)—they'd chuck the Monuments if they could dislodge them. They're so bent on mayhem, beer vendors have been instructed: "Please don't feed the Creatures" (who skirt the prohibition by tanking up before their arrival, right before game time).

Their streak of violent nihilism extends to inanimate objects, as illustrated by the Creature who not only grabbed a beach ball wafting across the stands, but pulled out his pocketknife and violently stabbed it while the other Creatures cheered.

Are they loud? A Toronto writer, accustomed to the

decorous murmuring of Blue Jays fans, said that one hundred Bleacher Creatures made more noise than a crowd of 20,000 at the SkyDome.

Then there's the "YMCA" chant. After the fifth inning of every Yankees home game, to the sounds of the Village People's "YMCA," the groundskeepers rake the infield until the chorus, when they drop their tools to lead the crowd in semaphoring the letters of the song. That the onetime gay anthem has become an innocent family ritual is an irony that seems lost on everyone concerned—except the Bleacher Creatures, who have "composed" substitute lyrics that return the song to its, um, rightful context. The new lyrics start, "Gay man, get up off your knees," and go downhill from there. As they sing, the Creatures "out" arbitrary victims in the crowd, which can lead to violent confrontation.

The Creatures are clannish, territorial, and, in their own macho, blue-collar way, self-important. They have their own Cesspool of Heroes such as Tina, Queen of the Bleachers, and Loudmouth Larry, whose idea of a witticism is yelling to the program vendor, "Yo! Give me a *Playboy*!"; their own version of a luxury box (they intimidate out-oftowners who have innocently stumbled onto their turf into migrating to other sections), and their own grunge version of Monument Park. After one bleacherite, Ali Ramirez, passed away in 1996, a gold plate was affixed to Seat 29, Row A, Section 39. It reads: THIS SEAT IS TAKEN IN THE MEMORY OF ALI RAMIREZ, THE ORIGINAL BLEACHER CREATURE. Ali's claim to fame? Banging a pan nonstop.

ONE-WAY LOYALTY:
HOW THE YANKEES SCREW THEIR FANS

Fans like this offer themselves to the team as a beer-bellied militia, and how does the Yankee organization treat them?

Well, first they shut them out of post-season tickets. For example, in 1999, only 5,000 out of 57,000 tickets for each World Series game were made available to the public; the rest were diverted to corporate cronies and influential politicos. To dispense the rest, the team has staged lotteries, but they've been quickly corrupted, as cops escort friends or the well connected to the front of the line.

This cavalier indifference to loyal customers goes way back in Yankee history. In the last game the team ever played in the Polo Grounds before moving to Yankee Stadium, against the Philadelphia Athletics, a mob desperate to see rising slugger Babe Ruth play long-ball stampeded the gate after it was announced that the game was sold out. One person was killed, dozens were injured, and parts of the park were torn to shreds. Less than 10 years later, on May 19, 1929, a severe mid-game rainstorm sent right-field bleacherites—the Ur-Creatures, as it were—dashing for the only exit the team had kept open. In this cattle run, two died and dozens more were injured. It was later discovered that owner Jacob Ruppert had kept the exits locked so he wouldn't have to give out rain checks.

It's not enough for the Yankee brass to squeeze every last dime from the loyalists; it also keeps the fans under such close surveillance—from police, private security, rooftop spy cameras, and the Orwellian Goodyear Blimp—it's as if they suspected Osama bin Laden was in the park and passing coded signs to al-Qaeda through their opponent's third-base coach.

The ultimate chutzpah? The Yankee management's longtime (and mostly empty) threat to move the team to Jersey. (See Chapter 6: Condemning the House That Ruth Built.)

Even the Fake Yankees Fans Suck

While the Yankees and MLB were awaiting the outcome of a court case arising from the team's decision to sign their lucrative marketing deal with Adidas, Bud Selig allowed the Yankees to run Adidas ads within the team's local region as long as no players were shown. Adidas's United States ad agency decided by necessity to organize a campaign around fans. So they created five fictional characters, the "ANSKY" guys, balding, endomorphic schlubs who jam into the backseat of a cab each wearing a letter of the word "YANKS" painted on his belly—only in their haste to squeeze into the taxi, they scramble their letters. The cabbie asks, "What the hell is Ansky?" A bit of slapstick ensues as they attempt to de-Scrabble themselves. The ads not only won a Clio award but one at the Cannes Film Festival (the Asshole d'Or). The ANSKY-ites also had their own float in the Yanks' Canyon of Heroes World Series parade.

Believe it or not, the Bleacher Creatures complained; they felt they deserved their own float, too.

NOTES

1. Robert Lipstye, *New York Times*.
2. Dean Chatwin, *Those Damn Yankees*.
3. John Kuenster, *Baseball Digest*, December 2000.
4. Ibid.

Chapter Four

THE MADNESS OF
KING GEORGE

He's every worker's nightmare, the satanic CEO; a fanatically controlling overlord who borrows his warmed-over rhetoric from Vince Lombardi and his managerial style from Stalin. He hogs all of the credit and assumes none of the blame. He humiliates his players by berating them in the press, apologizing to fans for losses, and posting "inspirational" messages—"When the going gets tough, the tough get going"—on the Diamond Vision scoreboard. He's a ruthless, acquisitive, hypocritical, obnoxious "turtlenecked gargoyle"[1]—in other words, the personification of the New York Yankees.

George Steinbrenner is the most visible and most influential owner in American team sports. He's also a convicted felon (and the first person to attain that status in connection with the Watergate burglary), an *opera buffo* villain (played as such by Larry David on *Seinfeld*), and a 74-year-old man who spends more time on Page Six than Britney Spears.

He prattles endlessly about "Yankee tradition" and how "winning is everything" and cites the wisdom of generals. Yet in reality, he's like every other bully—the first to back down if confronted, hit the panic button, and point the accusatory finger at everyone but himself. He dubs certain players "warriors," while he "spits the bit." Buster Olney, in his book, *The Last Night of the Yankee Dynasty*, records that in the eighth inning of Game 6 of the 2003 World Series, with the Yanks down, 2–0, Steinbrenner cornered general manager Brian Cashman. "Meeting in Tampa Monday," he snapped. "And it's not going to be pleasant. There are going to be big changes." *The game wasn't even over.* And in the bottom of the ninth in Game 7 of the 2001 World Series, after leadoff hitter Mark Grace dumped a single into centerfield, Steinbrenner turned to an undoubtedly mystified attendant in the visitors' clubhouse, jabbed a finger and said, "If we lose this, it's all your fault."

In his 31 years as Yankees owner, King George has run his team like a pinstriped dictatorship, hiring friends and cronies, buying politicians, and holding periodic purges. During his long, dysfunctional relationship with manager Billy Martin (see sidebar), he even conducted the baseball equivalent of show trials, in which the now-chastened manager would display public contrition for his unruly behavior and pledge eternal fealty to the pinstripes. Team executives are held under the baseball version of house arrest—he has punished Cashman by "grounding" him so he couldn't attend baseball's winter meetings, and once banned him from walking on the grass behind home plate, presumably because that would prevent him from talking to reporters.[2]

So omnipresent is his intimidation that even top lieutenants such as Mark Newman have been known to get down on their hands and knees to smooth a rug at the team's Tampa headquarters, for fear of contravening the Boss's demand for military perfection. ("Even when he's not here, he's here," Newman said, sounding like a North Korean peasant caught talking to a Western reporter.)

FrankenSteinbrenner instills a cultlike paranoia about losing by making endless late-night phone calls to employees and ordering them to remain at their office posts after losses. Some employees of the YES network, speaking to me off the record, said they often had to stay at work for several hours after night games, yet were expected back early the next morning. The impression I got was that hostages in Iraq had higher morale.

The threat of imminent dismissal hangs over the organization like the Asia cloud, and with good reason. Steinbrenner, a berserk headhunter, has changed managers 20 times in his first 23 seasons as owner (including firing Billy Martin five times and rehiring him four times) and general managers 11 times in his 31-year reign of terror. Coaches are demoted for having a runner thrown out at home,[3] and they serve as convenient scapegoats if their hitters, pitchers, and catchers don't meet George's impossible standards.

Steinbrenner, a former vice president of the United States Olympic Committee, wreathes himself in the flag. He hangs quotations from Douglas MacArthur at the team's Tampa training complex and often wears an Ol' Glory pin on his jacket lapel. The Yankees are the only major league team that plays "God Bless America" during every home game. He believes so much in American democracy that he was convicted for making illegal contributions to Richard Nixon's presidential campaign.

Steinbrenner's ham-fisted micromanaging has swayed the franchise between eras of rousing success and pratfalling ineptitude. In the 1970s, he pioneered in the acquisition of free agents Catfish Hunter and Reggie Jackson, and the team won two championships. In the 1980s, he signed busts such as Dave Collins and Danny Tartabull, and the team crashed and burned. It was only in the early 1990s, when he was sitting out his second suspension from baseball, that then-GM Gene Michael (who he had already fired as manager numerous times) and manager Buck Showalter had the freedom to lay the groundwork for the Joe Torre dynasty.

George once proudly declared, "I never have a heart attack. I give them." And he has—to employees, other owners, and Yankee fans—but then, they deserve it.

THE GEORGE STEINBRENNER STORY

George Steinbrenner grew up in suburban Cleveland, the son of a shipbuilder. His first jobs included coaching high school football and basketball in Columbus, Ohio. (Under some strange psychodynamic spell, George would later punish errant—and marginal—Yankees by exiling them to this city on what became known as the Columbus Shuttle. Utility infielder Randy Velarde was shuttled so frequently, he should've taken flying lessons.)

In 1956, Steinbrenner married Joan Zieg, who hasn't been heard from since and who may be imprisoned in a dungeon far below the Yankee Stadium bleachers, along with Ed Whitson and Bobby Meacham. The following year, he joined his father's struggling American Shipbuilding Company, from which he would make his millions before eventually running it aground. (It filed for bankruptcy protection in the early 1990s.) In 1960, Steinbrenner bought the Cleveland Pipers of the American Basketball League, a foreshadowing of more ambitious franchise conquests and the sports equivalent of Hitler seizing the Sudetenland. However, he was unable to raise enough money to join the NBA, and the Pipers went under.

His total ignorance of how to run a baseball team didn't curb his ambition to own one. In the early 1970s, he offered $9 million to buy the Cleveland Indians and was turned down. (Let's do some alternate history here: What if

George had owned the Indians instead of the Yankees? Without the revenues accrued from living in a large market, he would've probably mishandled the team out of existence, but not before blaming his failures on the "big market clubs," accusing Albert Belle of "jaking it" and having "Hillerich & Bradsby" permanently tattooed on his skull.)

In 1973 he assembled a group of private investors to purchase the New York Yankees from the Columbia Broadcasting System for $10 million. (The franchise is now estimated to be worth almost one hundred times that amount.) At the press conference, he said he would not be involved in the team's daily operations. (Hey, they believed Hitler when he said he wanted peace.) The palace intrigue began immediately. His first general partner quit after four months, the first of many defections from George's realm. One of his co-investors, John McMullen, said, "There is nothing more limited than being a limited partner of George Steinbrenner."

George entered baseball at the dawn of free agency, which he opposed—"I am dead set against free agency. It can ruin baseball," he proclaimed—until Oakland A's pitcher Jim "Catfish" Hunter was released from his contract in 1974. Then George anted up for the pitcher the unheard-of salary of $2.85 million for four years, a deal that raised the contractual bar and made enemies of his fellow owners.

Right after the Hunter deal, he was indicted for funneling money to Nixon. While Steinbrenner has always demanded unquestioned loyalty from his minions, before his conviction, he contemplated snitching to obtain a more lenient sentence, according to the website The Smoking Gun:

[In a] memo prepared by lawyers with the Watergate special prosecutor, Steinbrenner attorney Edward Bennett Williams said that his client had information on other illegal contributions, not to mention the sale of ambassadorships and a Teamsters slush fund. Steinbrenner, whose offer was rejected, eventually pleaded guilty to a felony conspiracy count as well as a misdemeanor charge. . . . For 15 years, he petitioned for a presidential pardon until Ronald Reagan gave it to him in 1989, two days before he left office.[4]

Commissioner Bowie Kuhn suspended Steinbrenner for two years. He later reduced the punishment to nine months, just in time for George to open the Bronx Zoo, the feuding, circus-like mid-'70s squad that staged more brawls than the WWF and had more drama queens than you'd find at Wigstock. George was omnipresent, ripping players, coaches, umpires, and league officials; second-guessing managers; and delivering rah-rah clubhouse diatribes. It seems a day didn't pass without Steinbrenner and/or some of his overpaid mercenaries catfighting on the back pages. And the staggering turnover of Yankee personnel throughout the late '70s led third baseman Graig Nettles to quip, "Every year is like being traded—a new manager and a whole new team."

Somehow, the team won, which drew out two distinctly Steinbrennerian traits: (1) he usurped all the credit for the team's success, when it was general managers Al Rosen and Gabe Paul who had made the trades for Graig Nettles, Mickey Rivers, Ed Figueroa, Chris Chambliss, and others; and (2) revealing his total lack of talent evaluation, he had pressured his front office to trade a future Yankee star—in this case, Ron Guidry. (Fifteen years later,

GM Gene Michael prevented him from trading the young Bernie Williams.) In the 1970s, the team won three pennants and two World Series, but why dwell on them? It's like reminding yourself of an ex-girlfriend who posted graphic details of your sexual inadequacy on Friendster.

George & Billy

Steinbrenner and Martin. Baseball's answer to George and Martha, an Albee-esque psychodrama played out on the back pages, full of fury and surreal, theater-of-the-absurd twists and turns that left even diehard Yankee fans stunned and bewildered and Yankee haters chortling with schadenfreude. George would fire Billy for public insults, drunken brawling, or insubordination, then magically rehire him. Here's a quick summation of the most twisted relationship in the history of American sports:

✦ July 24, 1978: With the Yankees far behind the first-place Red Sox, Martin lashes out at Reggie Jackson and Steinbrenner, "One's a born liar; the other's convicted." A few days later in Kansas City, a sobbing Martin reads a prepared statement in which he resigns as the Yankee manager.

✦ July 29, 1978: During Old-Timers Day at Yankee Stadium, it is announced that Martin will return to manage the Yanks in 1980, surprising players, fans, and especially Bob Lemon, who had just been named interim manager. Lame-duck Lemon leads the team from 14½ games out to win the pennant and World Series.

✦ October 28, 1979: After reassuming the helm a year earlier than what had previously been announced, Martin is fired by Steinbrenner again after the psychotic manager gets into yet another of his barroom brawls. Dick Howser is named to replace him.

✦ April 25, 1982: Just 14 games into the season, Steinbrenner fires Lemon and replaces him with Gene Michael, the man Lemon had replaced the previous September.

✦ January 11, 1983: Round 3— George hires Billy as manager, replacing Clyde King.

✦ December 16, 1983: Martin is fired again and given a front-office job. (This is another favorite ploy of Steinbrenner's, always keeping disgraced employees in liege to him.) Yogi Berra is named the new manager.

- April 28, 1985: After the Yankees lose to the White Sox 4–3 on a bases-loaded walk in the bottom of the ninth, Yogi is replaced by none other than Martin. George, ever the coward, makes ex-skipper-turned-pitching-coach King deliver the pink slip, and a furious Berra vows never to set foot in Yankee Stadium again as long as Steinbrenner is the owner.

- October 27, 1985: Martin is fired again, replaced by Lou Piniella.

- October 19, 1987: Piniella is replaced by Martin.

- June 23, 1988: Steinbrenner fires Martin for the fifth time, replacing him again with Lou Piniella.

By this time, the Billy & George act had gotten stale, like the road company of "The Sunshine Boys." Yet this strange codependency lasted until the end of Martin's life. When he crashed his car into a tree near his home in Fenton, New York on Christmas Day in 1989, he was working as a "special consultant" to Steinbrenner.

In the 1980s, King George seemed more interested in tabloid appearances than the success of his club, and his tyrannical interference wreaked havoc with the franchise. He was like a spoiled kid playing in a rotisserie league. There were defections of luminaries Goose Gossage, Nettles, and Jackson; mindless acquisitions of derelict stars (Steve Kemp, Jack Clark, Toby Harrah, Butch Hobson) and mediocrities (Whitson, John Mayberry, Mike Armstrong); impulsive, irrational firings (after manager Dick Howser was let go after a 103-win season and ALCS loss in 1980, Steinbrenner explained that "He's leaving to pursue a great real-estate deal in Florida"), the inept assembling of the stumbling 1982 "speed Yankees" that finished fifth, and a general atmosphere of fear and loathing in which Steve Trout couldn't find the plate with a divining rod and Whitson hyperventilated before each of his horrendous starts.

Despite having three Hall of Fame–worthy everyday

players (Dave Winfield, who was elected; Rickey Henderson, who will be, and Don Mattingly, who would've been if he hadn't hurt his back), the '80s were the first decade since 1910 in which the team didn't win a championship.

"BAD HOOKUP": THE HOWARD SPIRA INCIDENT

It sounds like a film noir plot: Owner signs free-agent superstar, grows disenchanted, is sued by the star over the funding of the free agent's nonprofit foundation, and looks to vengefully discredit him by paying an entry-level hoodlum—who had worked as the superstar's gofer until said star spurned his request to pay off a huge gambling debt—to dig dirt. James M. Cain, meet George M. Steinbrenner.

It was 1987, and the Yankees were spiraling into the division cellar. So what does Steinbrenner do? Launch a vendetta against Dave Winfield, who he had just traded to California after first giving the outfielder a 10-year, $15 million contract. The Boss blamed Winfield for the team's failure to win championships, derisively referred to him as "Mr. May," and refused to honor an agreement to pay $300,000 in annual donations to Winfield's charity, thereby instigating a series of bitter lawsuits.

Meanwhile, Howard Spira, a wormy little nonentity (who in the Hollywood biopic would've been played by Elisha Cook, Jr.) described as a "sycophantic errand boy" to Winfield, was begging the star to pay off certain creditors who didn't know the meaning of "debt consolidation." When Big Dave refused, sleazeball Spira approached Big George, who—astonishingly—paid him forty grand to be his personal truffle pig and root out any info that could damage Winfield's reputation.

In a classic plot twist, Spira turned from informer to extortionist and now demanded $110,000 from Mr. Bluster, who later insisted that he paid up because Spira "scared me, and he really scared my children." As it turned out, George had reason to be afraid: In July 1990, Commissioner Fay Vincent, dismissing the idea that the nebbish Spira could possibly be extorting from a multimillionaire power-broker, banned George from any hands-on operation of the Yankees. When the suspension was announced during a Yankee home game, all 24,000 fans gave it a standing ovation that lasted a full minute. It was perhaps the Yankee fans' greatest moment.

Vincent planned to suspend Steinbrenner for two years, but the latter, for reasons nobody can produce, asked for a lifetime ban. Was it a cry for help? ("Stop me before I trade Buhner for Phelps!") We may never know. Even after Spira was convicted of extortion—he got 2½ years—Vincent upheld George's suspension. With George out of the way—his son-in-law, team vice president Joseph Molloy, was appointed as the club's "acting" managing general partner— GM Gene Michael and other execs incubated the 1990s Yankee dynasty, secure in the knowledge that George couldn't panic-trade away their budding stars for the carcasses of washed-up free agents. Damn you, Fay Vincent!

The ban was lifted after three years, and later, when Steinbrenner was asked about the Spira incident, his response was, "Bad hookup. Bad hookup. There were reasons, but no reason would've been good enough to have done that...I wish Dave Winfield and I hadn't pulled apart." (When it came time for Winfield to enter the Hall of Fame, it was rumored that George tried to bribe him into wearing his Yankee cap. Winfield waltzed into Cooperstown as a San Diego Padre.)

THE BARREN YEARS

By the early 1990s, Steinbrenner had sunk the Yanks like one of his dad's battleships. The team was a mélange of stiffs and spare parts managed by a guy named Stump Merrill, who, after a clubhouse meal, cleaned his teeth with a game-used sock. Steinbrenner's malign treatment of Winfield and other players (as well as the team's disintegration) scared away free agents, who feared that sooner or later, regardless of their performance, George would turn on them. The team's fortunes only turned around when George, right before he went into suspended animation, hired Gene Michael as GM in 1991. Within two years, Michael had weeded out the malcontents like Mel Hall and boosted the team to a 88–74 record. Did George, after his reinstatement, appreciate the reconstruction job Michael had done? No way, according to Olney.

"This team is messed up," he told Michael. "The players are messed up; everything is messed up. This was in good shape when I left." Two years later, after the Yanks' first playoff appearance in 14 years, Mr. Bluster demoted Michael to scout. He continued to hog credit until the team lost, when he would blame his "baseball people." Bob Watson, who succeeded Michael as GM, was once asked who these "baseball people" were. "They're the little people who run around in his head," he replied. Within three years, Watson, his health shot by George's harassment, quit.

Of course, this was right in the middle of the dynasty, a really ugly period in Yankee Hater history, a seemingly endless loop of Jetes, Paulie, Torre, and the rest spraying champagne all over George's JV football coach windbreaker.

One wonders if the team's exceptional run was fueled more than anything else by the players' knowledge that the only thing that could keep Mt. Steinbrenner relatively dormant was *not losing*. But no team, not even the Yankees, with all their ill-gotten gains, can always win, and their failure to take home a championship in the past four years has led to the return of Evil George: the guy who makes veiled threats about the job security of his manager, supersedes his "baseball people" to acquire clubhouse malignancies such as Raul Mondesi, causes his GM, Brian Cashman, to grind his teeth to their nubs, and in a fit of petulance after the 2002 playoff loss to Anaheim, threatens to cut his employees' dental plan—in effect, sacrificing his employees' wisdom teeth for a half-season of Bubba Crosby. (The Boss backed down when his son Hal offered to pay the $150,000 out of his own pocket to save the plan.)

Steinbrenner is 74, seemingly kept alive, like a modern mummy, by the talismanic power of owning the Yankees. But there are signs that he's failing. In late 2003, while attending the funeral of the great Cleveland Browns quarterback Otto Graham, he collapsed. At the time it was attributed to his grief over his old pal. However, the real cause may have been the considerable stress George was in after receiving subpoenas from the New York State Lobbying Commission over free tickets given to area political officials. Four days later, the Yankees agreed to pay a $75,000 fine and turn over the names of politicians who had received tickets, curtailing any further investigation.

While he may survive long enough to see the fruits of those bribes—a new Yankee Stadium extorted from the city—eventually he'll pass over to the other side. (The image I have is him screaming, "You listen to me! I used to *own* the Devils!") The rest of us can take satisfaction that he'll spend eternity on the ultimate losing team. With Billy Martin as his manager.

THE FUTURE: WILL YOUNG ELEPHANTS LEAVE A COLOSSAL MESS?

Observers of the Yankees are unclear about the team's post-George future[5] and, much like Kremlinologists pondering the succession of Soviet leaders, can only speculate. The three candidates—who George calls "the young elephants"—are his two sons, Hank and Hal, and his son-in-law Steve Swindal, who's married to George's daughter, Jennifer. (His other daughter, Jessica, writes children's books. How about *The Little Engine That Spit the Bit*?)

It's been reported that George treated his kids like his father, Henry Steinbrenner, did him—with grandiose expectations, verbal abuse, and little love. According to his daughter, Jennifer, the Steinbrenner spawn were expected to excel at every childhood endeavor.[6] (You can just hear George screaming, "You call that potty training?")

Hank seems more interested in tending to his dad's horse-racing interests, while Hal is described as lacking the passion to run a big-league baseball team. This leaves Swindal, who married into the family business and likes to pilot tugboats.[7] (Maybe he could use one to tow Jason Giambi out to sea.)

George, who probably doesn't trust his own blood—why should he?—seems to prefer Swindal, who he tapped to negotiate Joe Torre's current contract.

While George could always sell the team, he has reportedly taken the necessary steps to slowly shift power to the elephants in a way that would ease the burden of inheritance taxes. In retirement, he might, like other major-league owners (e.g., George Argyros) who have contributed to George W. Bush's campaigns, expect to be appointed an ambassador, to a country like Italy. ("What you do mean, national strike? Get me Connors on the line!")

But for now, King George sits atop the throne of Yankee-dom, and—who knows?—he may be there forever. Author Neil DeMause speculates that "Steinbrenner spent his most recent two-year suspension being reanimated in a lab."

As long as Torre and Cashman are nominally in charge, the team should have relative stability. But what happens when they leave? The scuttlebutt among agents and major-league executives is that some players are wary of inking long-term pacts with the Yankees for fear of the climate once the manager and GM leave the team. If we cross our fingers, we'll see the late-1980s–early-1990s redux.

Perhaps George's greatest legacy is that he's created in his image—winning-obsessed, perpetually dissatisfied, impossibly demanding, paranoid, manic, and highly neurotic—a host of Mini Me's, who have all of those personality flaws without any of his money or power. They're called Yankee fans.

More George Lowlights

1. George bullied the Hall of Fame to elect undeserving shortstop-broadcaster-icon Phil Rizzuto by boycotting the Hall of Fame game. Since the plurality of HOF visitors are Yankee fans, the action carries some muscle, and the Veterans' Committee enshrined the Scooter and his cryogenically frozen cannolis.

2. You're fired! George taught his good buddy Donald Trump the meaning of the phrase with his impetuous mass dismissals. During the 1970s and 1980s, he fired an average of 30 employees per season. In 1996, Steinbrenner surpassed himself by canning 56 employees. Many of his replacements are family friends, whose appointments he justifies by declaring that he wants to promote "unity" within the backroom staff. The morning after the Yanks lost to the Florida Marlins in the 2003 World Series, Steinbrenner fired the first employee he came across in his Tampa headquarters. He's fired people so arbitrarily that he soon forgets he's done so. Lou Saban, Yankees president in 1981, recalls: "One night we were having a benefit for a police officer killed in the line of duty. George was in Tampa. I made a special presentation before the game. There was a full house, fifty-four thousand people. We're up five-zero in the third inning when the sky just opens up. It starts raining like I never could believe. My phone rings. It's George. He's not happy. He wants to know how it looks. 'The field is inundated,' I tell him. So he hangs up on me. Ten minutes later, the phone rings again. It's George. 'What's going on?'

'You know what's going on. It's pouring. Water is cascading into the dugouts.' He hangs up on me again. He calls two more times. He tells me to call the umpires and tell them to do everything they can to get the game in. He hangs up on me both times. The phone rings again. Guess who? He wants to know what's going on. I tell him it's still raining and looks terrible. 'Why didn't you know it was going to rain?' he says. 'George, I'm not the guy upstairs! I don't turn on the valves!' 'You're fired!' he says, and bang, hangs up the phone again. After the game got rained out, we went into George's office and drank up his liquor. I got home at four in the morning. At nine a.m. George is in his office in the Stadium asking Mary, my secretary, 'Where's Saban?' 'He's not here. You fired him last night.' 'What are you talking about? You tell him he better be in this office in an hour.' "[8]

3. The Phantom Elevator Fight. After the Yanks' third straight loss to the Dodgers in the 1981 World Series, Steinbrenner claimed that while in his hotel elevator, he "clocked" two Dodger fans who had taunted him by calling the Yanks "chokers" and then hit him over the head with a beer bottle. And yet, according to Murray Chass of the *New York Times*, nobody believed a word of George's story. There were no witnesses. Nobody came forward to sue him or even report the incident. "Despite a variety of injuries—a cast-covered left hand, scraped knuckles on his right hand, a bump on his head, a bloody lip—Steinbrenner failed to convince everyone that he really had engaged in a fight," Chass wrote.

4. Political shenanigans. Besides the illegal campaign contributions, George's insidious relations with New York City politicos, especially former mayor Rudy Giuliani, are a political hidden-ball trick. He gave Giuliani ample free advertising and electioneering time—even allowing him to do TV and radio interviews with the Yanks' broadcasters during games. He proffered free post-season tickets and wined and dined top city officials. And he hired as team president Randy Levine, the city's former deputy mayor for economic development (who was once a Yankee attorney and also worked for Major League Baseball). As one writer put it, "Helps to have a Steinbrenner pal in the mayor's inner sanctum when you're trying to get a new taxpayer-funded stadium, no?"

George Goes Bonkers:
A Peek Into the Future

Everybody knows we've hardly seen the last of Mt. Steinbrenner. Here are some explosions we're likely to see from the Yanks' blowhard owner:

1. After a loss to the Devil Rays, George orders Brian Cashman to eat dog food off the floor of his office. Cashman complies; it still beats Stadium hot dogs.

2. Yanks fall into second place. George orders grounds crew to perform "YMCA" routine wearing only thongs.

3. Relievers get hammered. Bullpen coach "disappeared."

4. Three-game losing streak. George has team physician undo em-

ployees' dental work; fillings are re-moved, root canals re-excavated.

5. After he runs out of players to get rid of, George picks out random fan from crowd and trades him to Kansas City.

6. George punishes a slumping A-Rod by locking him in a dank Stadium basement chained to John Sterling.

NOTES

1. Selena Roberts, *New York Times*, September 30, 2004.

2. "The Yankees Most Valuable Player," Chris Smith, *New York* magazine, September 2004.

3. The coach was Mike Ferraro, who in Game 2 of the 1980 ALCS against Kansas City, waved in Willie Randolph, who later occupied the same third-base coaching box.

4. From www.thesmokinggun.com/yankees/georgesnitch1. html.

5. Most of the information about the future of the team comes from "Life After the Boss," New York *Daily News*, late 2003.

6. Tampa Bay Business Journal, September 13, 1996. American Shipbuilding bought a Tampa tugboat operation, Marine Towing, in 2004 (source: *St. Petersburg Times*, April 28, 2004).

7. "Steinbrenner Aims to Put All His Houses in Order," Juliet Macur, *New York Times*, May 2, 2004.

8. Wayne Coffey, New York *Daily News*, www.nydailynews. com/sports/baseball/story/47460p-44621c.html.

Chapter Five

THE DARK SIDE OF
THE YANKEES

In Yankeeland, nobody lives but heroes, legends, and various kinds of Bronx nobility. The Yankee goats and chokers—like Politburo members fallen into disfavor—have been carefully airbrushed from the official history. But if you peer beneath the team mythology, you'll find a seamy underbelly of vice, corruption, and bigotry that extends back to the origins of the franchise.

CONCEIVED IN SIN

The Yankees would have you believe that the team sprung full-blown into glory in 1920 with the arrival of Babe Ruth from the Red Sox. However, the franchise came into existence originally as the Baltimore Orioles, and then the New York Americans (nicknamed the Highlanders, among other things) under extremely dubious circumstances in 1903.

A little background: At the turn of the twentieth century, there was only one major league, the National League of Professional Baseball Clubs, which was formed in 1876.[1] In 1899, the Western League (a minor league in the Midwest) aspired to major-league status and changed its name to the American League. After the 1900 season, its president, Ban Johnson, and three of the league owners, decided to move their teams into eastern cities to challenge the National League monopoly. They wanted to place one of the new clubs in New York City, but they were stymied by the National League owners, who had strong political ties to the Tammany Hall Democratic machine that had run New York for most of the nineteenth century. The franchise instead was placed in Baltimore, whose National League club had folded the previous year when the league contracted. In 1902, Andrew Freedman, the owner of the New York Giants, bought the Orioles and raided the team for players (a very common occurrence in the Gay Nineties era of "syndicate" ownership). In response to this, Johnson and the league took over the Baltimore franchise, still planning to move them to New York.

According to David Pietrusza, author of *Major Leagues: The Formation, Sometimes Absorption and Mostly Inevitable Demise of 18 Professional Baseball Organizations, 1871 to Present* (McFarland & Co., 1991), Johnson found a promising site bordered by 142nd and 145th streets, Lenox Avenue and the Harlem River. The new site was also near a new station of the Interborough Rapid Transit subway. Johnson's agents convinced John B. McDonald, an IRT contractor, to purchase the land and lease it to the American League. McDonald then persuaded financier August Belmont II to come aboard. However, an IRT director—one Andrew Freedman—soon killed the plan.

In early 1902, the estate of Josephine Peyton auctioned off 12 parcels of land for $377,800 to John J. Byrne, a nephew of "Big Bill" Devery, who was an active Democrat in Manhattan's Ninth District, a blatantly corrupt New York City police chief who had been forced out of the department a month earlier, and one of the city's most notorious gamblers.

As Pietrusza tells it:

Devery soon was in business with Frank Farrell, another major operator. Ex-saloonkeeper Farrell owned 250 pool halls in the city and was closely connected to "Boss" Sullivan, an even greater star in New York's underworld firmament. Coal dealer Joseph Gordon, acting as front man for Farrell and Devery, approached Johnson, telling him his group could easily arrange for a park to be built if given a franchise. Devery and Farrell paid $18,000 for the Baltimore franchise and installed Gordon as president. Devery's name was missing from those listed as stockholders, although it was well-known he had contributed approximately $100,000 to the enterprise.

"Me a backer!" Devery modestly, if somewhat dishonestly, exclaimed. "I only wished I did own some stock in a baseball club. I'm a poor man and don't own stock in anything. Besides, how could I pitch a ball with this stomach?"

In another version of the story, as reported by

sportswriter Frank Graham, Johnson and his new ownership group were brought together by the *New York Sun*'s Joe Vila. Vila had known Johnson since the A.L. president's own sportswriting days and introduced him to Frank Farrell. Farrell was more than eager to purchase the Baltimore franchise, although Johnson was unsure about his prospective new club owner. His reticence evaporated when Farrell produced a $25,000 check and handed it over to Johnson, proclaiming, "Take this as a guarantee of good faith. If I don't put this ballclub across, keep it." "That's a pretty big forfeit," replied an amazed Johnson. "He bets that much on a horse race, Ban," Vila informed him. In any case the deal was made between the American League and its somewhat shady triumvirate. For $75,000 in actual construction costs (plus $200,000 in excavating the rocky, hilly terrain) a rickety, wooden, 16,000-seat park was constructed. A local Democratic politico, Thomas McAvoy, received contracts for both phases. On May 30, 1903, the Highlanders opened before 16,243 fans and defeated Washington 6–2 behind "Happy Jack" Chesbro.[2]

To help shore up the weak Highlander roster (which had finished last in Baltimore), Johnson waved big bucks at famous names such as Brooklyn outfielder "Wee Willie" Keeler. "I signed Keeler myself," boasted Johnson, "and I found him an easy man to deal with." The strengthened club finished a respectable fourth in 1903.

Let's see: shady owners conspiring with city officials to enable a franchise and build a new stadium, then enticing high-priced talent away from contending clubs. Sound familiar?

PINSTRIPES AND BLACK SOX[3]

They called him Prince Hal, but he was more like the Prince of Darkness. Hal Chase was considered by his peers to be the greatest fielding first baseman of his era. Yet although his career ended in 1918, he still holds the AL career first baseman's mark for errors (285) and led the league in that category seven times. How could this be? Real simple: Chase was a crook; he threw more games than Cy Young, betting against his own team for quick scratch. The Highlanders were one stop on his tour of venality. After the 1907 season, Chase held out for a $4,000 salary. After management gave it to him, he had the temerity to jump to San

Jose of the California League, where he played under an assumed name. New York suspended, then reinstated him. In the long Yankee tradition of patronizing sociopaths, when he returned, Chase's teammates presented him with a silver loving cup (which he probably pawned). In 1910 manager George Stallings accused Chase of throwing games. Chase not only beat the charge, he somehow used his evil charisma to become the team's player-manager at season's end. In his first full year, the team dropped from second place to sixth. In 1911, Chase resigned as manager, replaced by Harry Wolverton. (Those Ur-Yankees also went through a manager per year.) In 1913, manager Frank Chance accused Chase of "playing below his capability" (e.g., tanking games) and traded him to the White Sox. In 1918, playing for the Cincinnati Reds under the scrupulously honest Christy Mathewson, Chase was suspended for throwing games. According to the excellent website, www.baseballlibrary.com, "He was initially cleared by an establishment eager to disbelieve Chase's accusers, but the charge was later proven. John McGraw of the Giants, always sure of his ability to reform the wayward, tried Chase in 1919, but by the end of the season wouldn't play him." Chase's pièce de résistance was to come: He helped throw the 1919 World Series as a member of the infamous Chicago "Black Sox." The Highlanders/Yankees were a bad team during that era. When Prince Hal took the field, they were also a crooked one.

THE HOMICIDAL YANKEE

On August 16, 1920, Cleveland shortstop Ray Chapman dug in at the plate against Yankees submarine hurler Carl Mays. One of Mays's pitches froze Chapman and hit him squarely in the temple (which was unprotected by a batting helmet; they weren't used until years later). Chapman crumpled to the ground and died the next day, the sole on-field fatality in the history of major league baseball.

While Mays certainly didn't have homicidal intent, he was known as a nasty, intimidating pitcher who hunted more heads than a tribe of Amazonian cannibals. Mays's reputation was smirched but, true Yankee that he was, he brushed off the incident as an occupational hazard. A week later, he shut out Detroit, 10–0, and he went on to have the best seasons of his career. He pitched for nine more years, winning 207 games with a .622 winning percentage, although he, too, was suspected of throwing World Series games against the New York Giants in 1921 and 1922. He lived to the ripe old age of 79. Proving that homicide is contagious, one of Mays's teammates from the 1922–1923 Yankees, Bullet Joe Bush, was sued for killing a man in an auto accident.[4]

THE NEW YORK WHITE YANKEES[5]

When the Yankees were on the road in the 1930s and 1940s, the House That Ruth Built didn't stand empty. Besides prize fights, college and pro football games, and religious convocations that filled the place, a Negro League team called the New York Black Yankees, originally owned by tap-dance legend Bill "Bojangles" Robinson, played some of its home games there.

Yet until 1955, an occasional appearance by Satchel Paige or Cool Papa Bell was as close as Yankee management would get to acknowledging blacks, either on the field or in the stands. Even in a time of segregated baseball, the Yankees were known as the whitest of the white, and even after Jackie Robinson broke the color line, one writer called the club "the most notorious bastion of the tradition of white baseball in the post-1947 era."

During the 1930s and early 1940s, the most prominent bigot was team president Larry McPhail, a vicious alcoholic who socialized with mobsters such as Lucky Luciano, and actively resisted the major leagues' attempt to integrate. While McPhail, owner Jacob Ruppert, and general manager Ed Barrow rigidly toed the color line and constructed an image of haute bourgeois gentility, they had no compunction about signing nasty racists such as Jake Powell if they thought they could improve the team. Powell, an outfielder whose hitting in the 1936 World Series helped the Joe McCarthy—helmed team to the first of four straight championships, was a one-man Klan. In 1935, he broke Tiger first baseman Hank Greenberg's wrist. He constantly fought with other players, particularly those not white enough for his tastes. He went over the top in a July 29, 1938 postgame radio interview, in which he told broadcaster Bob Elson that in his off-season job as a policeman, he "beat up [ni**ers] and threw them in jail." Amid the national outrage that followed, Powell claimed that he had fabricated the incident, but Commissioner Kenesaw Mountain Landis suspended him for 10 games. From there it was all downhill, and ten years later, Powell shot and killed himself in a Washington, D.C., police station while being questioned on a bad-check charge. He's one guy you won't be seeing on "Yankeeography."

The team's plantation mentality continued even after the truculent McPhail was dismissed and Jackie Robinson broke the color line in 1947. Under the new ownership partnership of Del Webb and Dan Topping, the Yanks—who continued to win—increasingly drew their fans from affluent, white suburbs. George Weiss, who succeeded McPhail as GM, had this in mind when he said, "I will never allow a black man to wear the Yankee uniform. Box-holders from Westchester don't want that kind of crowd. They would be offended to have to sit with [ni**ers]." The Yanks' traveling secretary of the time, Bill McCorry, promised to keep all "[ni**ers]" off his trains.

And so, while their local rivals the Dodgers and Giants were signing the first wave of black superstars, the Yankees stood pat. They were one of the last clubs in baseball to integrate—this despite being one of the first clubs to sign black players. In 1949 Weiss recruited Artie Wilson, Frank Austin, and Luis Angel Martinez, and bought the contracts of Bob Thurman and Earl Taborn from the Kansas City Monarchs. But none of these black players came close to making the big club, and it was obvious that the signings were just PR moves. Jules Tygiel wrote in *Baseball's Great Experiment*:

In the post-1951 era, the Yankees recruited few additional prospects. Located in New York with a large black population and an active sporting press, the Yankee situation came under more stringent scrutiny than other clubs. As the years passed with no blacks added to the squad, even Dan Daniel, a devoted defender, often accused of being on the Yankee payroll, admitted, "If the Yankees weren't guilty as charged, they were certainly going out of their way looking for trouble."

It was only in 1955, eight years after Robinson broke in with Brooklyn, that a black player took the field in a Yankee uniform: the excellent but slow-footed catcher Elston Howard. His promotion led manager Casey Stengel to remark, "They finally got me a [ni**er], and he's the only one who can't run."

Even after Howard was brought on board, the team passed on one budding black superstar after another. Some baseball historians claim that the Yanks could've fielded a mid-50s outfield in which Willie Mays and Henry Aaron joined Mickey Mantle. The team also failed to promote the players it signed, such as Howard (who had been signed in 1950), and the velvet-gloved first baseman Vic Power. The first Puerto Rican signed by the team, Power was a black man who led the American Association in hitting in 1953. However, the following year, he was passed over while white Moose Skowron was promoted. As Dean Chatwin writes in *Those Damn Yankees: The Secret Life of America's Greatest Franchise*, "Topping's excuse was that Power couldn't field, yet when he did make the majors, with the Philadelphia (and then Kansas City) Athletics and other clubs, he won seven Gold Gloves with his innovative, stylish play and is considered by some experts to be the greatest fielding first baseman of all time." In fact, Power was so athletic that he was played at second base at numerous times during his career. Some observers speculated that the Yanks took a dim view of Power having a white wife. But this was not only bigoted, but inaccurate: Power's wife wasn't white.

After CBS bought the Yankees from Webb and Topping in 1964 and through the Steinbrenner era that began in 1973, the team has fielded a more racially diverse club. However, the team's commitment to multicultural tolerance is questionable. For one thing, for years Steinbrenner and his minions derogated the Yankee Stadium neighborhood, hoping to create a climate conducive to moving the team from the Bronx and/or getting a sweet new stadium deal from the city. For example, in 1991, Richard Kraft, George's college roommate and—believe it or not—the team's VP for community relations, told reporters that too many undesirables haunted the Stadium and that the team wanted to move away from these "monkeys." After a hailstorm of public outrage, George had to fire Kraft.

Even today, while the Yankees' attendance is at an all-time high, it still reflects the demographics of New York in 1960—mostly white suburbanites, who are also estimated to comprise a large portion of the YES network's TV audience. So, although Steinbrenner has failed (so far) to move the team physically, he has in effect shifted it to the virtual suburbs.

PINSTRIPED GOODFELLAS[7]

The Yankees like to promote their players—especially their superstars—as dignified, upstanding citizens. But throughout Yankee history, some of the walking Monuments cavorted openly with mobsters.

Let's start with the Yankee Clipper, Joe DiMaggio, who told rackets investigators in 1961 of his friendship with Albert "The Mad Hatter" Anastasia, a Murder, Inc. member who he had met only weeks before Anastasia was gunned down under orders of Carlo Gambino in the barber shop of the Park Sheraton Hotel in New York. When New York City police discovered the DiMaggio-Anastasia connection, they interrogated "the world's greatest living ballplayer" about his ties to non-baseball hit men such as Paul "Skinny" D'Amato, club owner, convict, and, according to the FBI, member of "La Cosa Nostra," and gambler Joseph Silesi, a partner of Florida mob boss Santo Trafficante, who some conspiracy theorists later implicated in the JFK assassination.

Joe D. told the Feds that he turned down an offer from Silesi to front for a gambling operation in Cuba because, "due to my image in the eyes of the American youth, I can't venture into gambling, whiskey, and cigarette endorsements."[5] DiMaggio then spent the rest of his life peddling banks, coffee machines, and parts of himself. (See Chapter 6: Condemning the House That Ruth Built.)

Number 5 wasn't the only Yankee who enjoyed the company of wiseguys. According to FBI files, members of the 1972 club also palled around with a mobster who, while in Florida to "establish connections with record bootleggers," gave the alibi that he was there "to frequent the training camp of the New York Yankees and renew many close associations he had with Yankee ballplayers." (The mobster's identity was redacted from the document.)

TRADING SPOUSES, THE YANKEE WAY

The late 1960s and early 1970s are remembered for drugs, demonstrations, and assassinations. Mores were changing overnight, and the sexual revolution even penetrated the cloistered, conservative world of the New York Yankees. After the 1972 season, Yankee pitchers Mike Kekich and Fritz Peterson scandalized the baseball world by swapping wives, kids, homes, and even dogs in a multi-player swap that even Bowie Kuhn couldn't stop. (To this day, it is not known if the wives had to clear waivers.)

Perhaps even stranger than the actual swapmeet was Peterson's earnest plea that the press "not make anything sordid out of this." Steinbrenner, who was in the process of purchasing the team from CBS, played indignant reactionary to the left-handed flower children. "When I first saw the team picture, it looked like a poster for birth control," the Boss absurdly raved to the New York *Daily News*. The Kekich-and-Marilyn Peterson-arrangement didn't work out, but Peterson and Susanne Kekich married and had four kids of their own. Peterson worked in real estate for a time, then found religion and became an evangelist. Neither Peterson nor Kekich ever made an appearance on Old-Timers Day.

THE HALFWAY HOUSE THAT RUTH BUILT

By the early 1990s, Steinbrenner had muted his moral outrage and accepted the Twelve-Step, disease model for what had in bygone eras been labeled as moral degeneracy. Either that, or his feverish drive for winning led him to dispense with any scruples about players' character. The result was the Halfway House That Ruth Built, and reliever Steve Howe cut the blue ribbon. The 1983 Rookie of the Year, former Dodger, and cocaine addict had already spent more time on the suspended list than Bart Simpson when Steinbrenner signed him to a minor-league deal in 1991.

But Howe couldn't get halfway through the next season before getting busted in Montana (what better place for snow-blowing?) after purchasing a gram. When Howe violated a drug-aftercare program, the lefty racked up a record seventh suspension and became the first player ever to be given a lifetime ban for substance abuse, only to be reinstated a few months later when arbitrator George Nicolau argued that the pitcher depended on the cocaine for helping him with his Attention Deficit Disorder. The Yankees, apparently suffering from the same disorder, re-signed Howe, who actually had a good year as their closer in 1994 before flopping and being released in 1996. Two days after his termination, he was found with a loaded gun in his suitcase at JFK airport. In 1999, Howe, who by now had seen more nose candy than Pablo Escobar, was banned because of substance abuse from volunteer coaching for his daughter's softball team. He appealed the ban and was rejected—proving that a girls' softball league has bigger *cojones* than the Yankees.

The most famous star in "Panic in Monument Park" is Darryl Strawberry.[8] By the time he signed with the Yanks in 1996, he had been treated for alcoholism, beaten both of his wives, and spent more time in Betty Ford than Gerry. Yet the sweet-swinging Strawberry helped the Bombers to their first title in almost 20 years. After missing two seasons with a knee injury and colon cancer, and while attempting a comeback in April 1999, Strawberry was arrested in Tampa for cocaine possession and soliciting an undercover officer for sex. Strawberry contended that the solicitation was some sort of reality-TV joke and that he didn't own the coke; he was given a four-month suspension by MLB. Three months after returning to help the Yankees win a second straight world championship, Strawberry again tested positive for cocaine and was suspended for a year. After a hospital stay, he was sentenced to spend two years in Phoenix House, a drug treatment center, but was ejected for breaking its rules, including the one against having sex with another resident. (He was married at the time.) Sentenced to 18 months for violating his probation, Strawberry was released in April 2003 from the Gainesville (Florida) Correctional Institution after serving 11 months. Even after Strawberry had assembled a rap sheet fit for a rap star, Steinbrenner hired him again in late 2003 as a spring-training instructor, a position Darryl left so he could devote himself to the Without Walls International Church, an evangelical religious institution that was "birthed in 1991" and offers "online tithing" on its website.

Strawberry's chief competitor for the wasted-youth award has to be Dwight Gooden.[9] The back of his baseball card might read:

1987: Drug rehab after testing positive for cocaine.

1987–1994: In and out of rehab so many times, the clinic puts in turnstiles just for him.

1994: Commissioner Bud Selig suspends him for the rest of 1994 and all of 1995. The day after the suspension, Doc seriously considers pulling the trigger of the nine-millimeter gun he holds to his head.

1996: George signs him, and he goes 11–7 and pitches a no-hitter against the Mariners. He hits 95 mph on the radar gun, after which Steve Howe asks if Dwight will recommend him to his dealer.

2000: After Gooden has bounced around with the Astros, Indians, and Devil Rays, the Yankees take yet another chance on him. Once again, he helps them win a World Series, with playoff victories in both the ALDS and ALCS.

2001: Gooden, along with ex-Met teammate Sid Fernández, tries to make the Yankees in spring training; they both fail. While in Florida, they stay with Sidd Finch, who owns a strip club in Tampa.

Despite his financial and marital problems, the Yankees continue to keep Gooden on the payroll. His current title is "special assistant." In October of 2003, Gooden's 17-year-old son, Dwight Eugene Gooden, Jr., was arrested for selling crack cocaine to undercover deputies in Tampa. He was given probation, and Steinbrenner promised him that if he could keep his nose dirty, he will always have a job with the New York Yankees.

KIDS ON DECK:
THE LUIS POLONIA RAPE CASE

On August 16, 1989, at the nadir of modern Yankee history, outfielder Luis Polonia was arrested in his hotel room in Milwaukee for having sex with a 15-year-old girl. He was sentenced to 60 days in prison after pleading no contest. A Solomon-like judge allowed Polonia to finish the season with the team, thus punishing the Yankees, since Polonia was one of the worst ballplayers in modern history—he had an on-base percentage around .300 and was a poor outfielder with a weak arm. Presumably, rape and general incompetence weren't sufficient to have him permanently banned from Yankee Stadium, for the Yanks brought him back not once, but twice—in 1995 and 2000.

LOCKER ROOM HOMOPHOBIA:
THE PAUL PRIORE INCIDENT[10]

In 1996, Paul Priore was a Yankee assistant equipment manager. His duties included straightening up the bat rack, washing uniforms, and ironing jockstraps—for which he was paid $30 a day. In August 1997, the team accused Priore of embezzlement—they believed he stole players' worn T-shirts, baseballs, and broken bats that were to be thrown away—and fired him (although they never pressed charges). In 1998, Priore filed a $50 million lawsuit alleging that Yankee pitchers Jeff Nelson, Bob Wickman (who by then was with Cleveland), and Mariano Rivera had taunted him and called him "faggot," and that Wickman had waved his penis in his face. (Where's that face mask when you need it?)

Priore claimed that the Yankees had discovered that he was HIV-positive and sought a pretext under which to fire him. A lower court ruled that the case could proceed to trial, but the New York State Supreme Court's Appellate Division unanimously reversed the ruling, saying there was no evidence that team officials knew that Priore had HIV. The team dentist who had treated Priore testified that he didn't know Priore was HIV-positive, and Yankee management said Priore had never complained about any harassment while with the team. The homophobia incident assumed a striking irony a few years later, with the introduction of the grounds crew's "YMCA" routine.

CRIMES AGAINST NATURE: WINFIELD'S SEAGULL

In the not-so-grand history of the Yankees, players and executives had gambled, drunk, drugged, whored, raped, partied with mobsters and cheated on their wives. On August 4, 1983, they created cross-species mayhem. While warming up before the fifth inning of the team's 3–1 win over the Blue Jays at Toronto's Exhibition Stadium, left fielder Dave Winfield accidentally killed a seagull with a thrown ball. After the game, Winfield was brought to the Ontario Provincial Police station on charges of cruelty to animals and forced to post a $500 bond before being released. Although the charges were dropped the next day, Winfield was booed every time the team played in Toronto.

NOTES

1. Some researchers contend that the National Association (1871–75) deserves consideration as the first major league

due to the caliber of player and level of play exhibited. However, game and individual records for the league weren't kept in a consistent manner. (Source: www.Wike pedia.com.)

2. By permission of David Pietrusza to the author.

3. Most of the material on Chase is from www.baseball-library.com.

4. Source: *The Sporting News*, June 15, 1916 (vol. 62, issue 15).

5. "Josh Gibson and Yankee Stadium," David Marasco, www.thediamondangle.com.

6. Most of the material from this section is adapted from *Those Damned Yankees: The Secret Life of America's Greatest Franchise* by Dean Chatwin (Verso Books, 1998).

7. The DiMaggio–mob material is taken from www.the smokinggun.com.

8. The Strawberry material is taken mostly from www.baseballlibrary.com.

9. Gooden material is taken mostly from www.baseball-library.com.

10. *Those Damn Yankees* by Dean Chatwin.

Chapter Six

CONDEMNING THE HOUSE THAT RUTH BUILT

"If you build it, they shall graft."

Yankee Stadium is the den of baseball iniquity, the corporate headquarters of the Evil Empire, and the lair of 57,478 bloodthirsty celebrants of a cult of *über*-free agents who pack the place from April until October. No wonder New Englanders call it *"Stade Fasciste."*

While it's one of only three prewar major league ballparks, the club and its fans would have you believe it's a national shrine—some combination of Valhalla and the Alamo. But is the House That Ruth Built really so special?

Monument Park

A thumbnail glance at the drunks, whoremongers, and racists the Yankees honor in their open-air mortuary:

Babe Ruth: Drank, ate, and wenched to wretched excess. Fathered illegitimate child. Protected by the press.

Lou Gehrig: Unnaturally devoted to his mother.

Joe DiMaggio: Nasty, vain, greedy; beat his wives, neglected friends, family, even his son ("While the old man was making a quarter-million dollars per weekend, signing baseballs, Joe DiMaggio, Jr., was living in a dumpster in California," says biographer Richard Ben Cramer[2]); in exchange for making personal appearances at mobsters' nightclubs, he accepted gifts from them, including a trust account at the Bowery Bank set up by Frank Costello that eventually netted DiMaggio over $1 million.[3]

Mickey Mantle: Drunk, serial adulterer, gambled on baseball.

Reggie Jackson: Pathologically self-aggrandizing egomaniac. Born Reginald Martínez Jackson—which led teammate Mickey Rivers to mock, "Your first name's white, your second is Hispanic, and your third belongs to a black. No wonder you don't know who you are"—Reggie was like George's lhasa apso, who he favored over mutts like Billy Martin and catcher Thurman Munson.

Billy Martin: Violent, psychopathic alcoholic.

Whitey Ford: Notorious for cheating by scuffing up balls.

Colonel Jacob Ruppert (owned

team from 1915 to 1939): Corrupt U.S. congressman; lifelong bachelor who designed Yankees' pinstriped uniforms[4]; in the closet?

Ed Barrow: Racist general manager.

GETTING THERE

Getting into the Green Zone is easier than accessing Yankee Stadium, due to the already sclerotic network of highways, throughways, "expressways," and bridges that encircle the place. And once you arrive, you'll end up paying a glorified car jockey half your kid's tuition for a space so far away from the Stadium, you'll need a GPS to find your seat. If you're in the city, the subway is quicker, but then you'll be packed into a metallic car thrumming underground at 50 miles per hour with hundreds of Yankee fans, and should you be wearing a Red Sox cap, you will end up on the third rail.

TICKET PRICES

The Yankees have the highest ticket prices in baseball except for the Red Sox, who with 22,000 fewer seats, really have no choice.

STADIUM ACCESS

Once you've secured your ticket, don't even think of bringing, well, almost anything into the stadium. Security guards, under orders from Uncle George, confiscate all banners critical of the team.

On its website, the team states:

> Due to increased security measures, in conjunction with Major League Baseball directives, the Yankees are instituting the following procedures: No backpacks, briefcases, attaché cases, coolers, glass or plastic bottles, cans, large purses, bags or video cameras will be permitted into the ballpark.* You must leave these items in your vehicle before entering the ballpark.

---

*Yankee security once confiscated from me a small cardboard box of fruit juice . . . this while selling more alcohol than Ernest and Julio Gallo.

If you don't have a "vehicle," you can check any such items with one of the numerous enterprising, quasi-legal baggage checkers who have sprung up near the Stadium. Among other items that terrorists may presumably use to wreak havoc: "Blow horns and all other distracting noise makers, laser pens/pointers, and beach balls." (Can't you just see an al-Qaeda operative shining that laser in A-Rod's face? "Proceed to the K Corner, infidel!") There's even an official Yankee-fan dress code, which prohibits "muscle T-shirts, sleeveless undershirts, tank tops, flip-flop shoes, and shorts above mid-thigh."

What's allowed? "Small children's backpacks, small women's purses and backpack purses, and diaper bags." Tip to Yankee Haters: If you want to sneak in an anti-Yankee banner, scrawl it on your kid's Pampers.

STADIUM AMENITIES

Yankee Stadium is considered a baseball temple; why, then, does it look like the lobby of an SRO hotel? One reason, says author Dean Chatwin, is the lousy concessions and lavatory facilities. "George terminated a contract with the service company that did a good job—they also serviced Shea Stadium—when the employees' union asked for a living wage," he says. So, as anyone who's attended a Yankees game knows, "the bathrooms reek of urine and the toilets go out of order after only a few innings."

All Along the Watchtower

Over the years, the Stadium has hosted not just baseball, but championship prize fights, Papal masses, and soccer matches. But the all-time attendance record was set not by a Yankees–Dodgers World Series game or Joe Louis vs. Max Schmeling, but by the Jehovah's Witnesses. As many as 123,707 of them convened in a single day there during the 1950s.

Another fan described conditions in the stands as no better: "It's absolutely filthy. By the fifth inning, heaps of garbage overflowed from huge bins under the bleachers, and it didn't look much better in the rest of the stadium. Steinbrenner has let the Stadium go to seed."

YANKEE CUISINE

What can you say about Yankee Stadium food? Styrofoam peanuts. Fossilized pretzels. Eight-dollar beer with all of the botulism and none of the taste. Jeff Marron, writing on ESPN.com, says of the overpriced frankfurter-manques:

A friend volunteered to eat a couple. The next day he got sick. On the subway home, I got to talking with another fan who sat in the loge boxes on the left-field side. He said he ordered a hot dog with sauerkraut at one stand near his seat. This left the concessionaires befuddled. They told him that if he wanted sauerkraut, he'd have to go to a hot dog stand on the other side of the stadium.

Jesus, the last time anybody rationed sauerkraut was in the Warsaw Ghetto.

Five Reasons Why New Yorkers Should Hate Yankee Stadium

The stadium refurbishment in the mid-1970s cost $180 million; the proposed new stadium will cost the city $450 million. Here are some municipal improvements the city can make if they let the Bombers go elsewhere.

1. $110 million for a program for dislocated workers cut from federal aid.

2. $240 million to replace money cut from the federal budget to fight poverty.

3. $50 million to improve public housing.

4. $20 million to help implement a new election law.

5. $20 million to help restore cuts to bioterrorism funds.

As for the nachos—for which, inexplicably, there are interminable lines—a neighbor of Marron's put it this way: "I ate a piece of my napkin with my nachos, and I didn't notice."

CONTRIVED SPONTANEITY

You would think that having a dynastic, perennially contending team and a collection of All-Stars would be enough to captivate Yankees fans. Not so. As if they were lemmings looking for a cliff, the organization insists on stage-managing every nanosecond of the fans' attention. The scoreboard impels them to clap, cheer, and boo. It distracts them with "subway races," in which colored icons representing New York underground lines "race" while the fans—undoubtedly with action riding on it—scream things like, "Eat me, six-train!"

To remind fans that there are higher causes than laying odds on a predetermined video game, the crowd is overdosed on patriotism, first with "The Star-Spangled Banner," then, during the seventh-inning stretch, with a version of "God Bless America" by Kate Smith or Irish tenor Ronan Tynan. For 12 years, John Luhrs, a scoreboard "character generator" (responsible for compiling stats to be flashed on DiamondVision), lurched to the Rednex tune "Cotton Eye Joe" like a cowboy with a neurological disorder—much to the Yankee fans' delight.

While Sinatra's post-game "New York, New York" was an inspired choice, the team has on occasion shifted to Liza Minnelli's version, a decision that can only be explained as a desperate attempt to market baseball to the Hedda Lettuce crowd.

A THREAT OR A PROMISE?
SHUT UP AND MOVE TO JERSEY

Although the Stadium was built in 1923, the current version is really only 30 years old. That's because in 1973–74, the original park was "modernized"—that is, almost completely torn down and rebuilt, during which its once-cavernous dimensions (it was 463 feet to dead center field) were drastically reduced and the monuments moved from the field of play to an area beyond the center-field fence now called "Monument Park." (The team played its home games at Shea Stadium for those two years.) According to author Neil DeMause, the renovation, originally estimated at $19 million, ended up costing the city $129 million. "At

New Yankees Promotions

To combat the Red Sox' innovative revenue streams—such as leading tour groups through Fenway Park—the Yankees have devised a list of new promotions:

1. George Steinbrenner available to haunt your children's Halloween party.

2. Fan Depreciation Day. Yanks' owner is allowed to write off entire crowd for tax purposes. All fans in attendance must sign a release confirming that they were not as loyal as they had been the previous year.

3. Anabolic Giambi Bobblehead Night. All fans 18 and over receive Jason Giambi bobblehead doll. Treat with clear or creamy substances and watch it grow.

4. "Outing" Night. Closeted homosexuals 18 and over are identified by public-address announcer Bob Sheppard, and their pictures are shown on DiamondVision.

5. Kiss Jeter's Rings Day. All fans are allowed to kiss Derek Jeter's four World Series rings and request miracles from Joe Torre.

6. Michael Kay Hostage Night. Fan drawing winning ticket gets to take Michael Kay home and lock him in a closet. Kay then is allowed one Cingular call to the bullpen to plead for his life.

7. Vegan Day. All vegan fans are fed to the Bleacher Creatures.

8. Fear Factor Night. Fans have eyelids taped open as Yanks' middle relievers enter game.

the time, the club promised that some of the Stadium funds would go for public services, but none of it did."[1]

Not content with a fully renovated home, Steinbrenner began clamoring for a spanking new one less than 10 years later, intimating that the Bronx environs were a perilous deterrent to fans. Yet almost 4 million fans attended games there in 2004—a team record—and due to a police-security presence fit for a G8 summit, the Stadium neighborhood is the safest place in the Bronx on game nights.

During the mid-1980s and for more than a decade thereafter, as the expiration of the Yankees' lease with the city (the landlord of Yankee Stadium) approached, Steinbrenner periodically threatened to move the team, first to New Jersey, then to the west side of midtown Manhattan. As Chatwin wrote in *Those Damn Yankees*:

Steinbrenner's people and the Boss himself engaged in a campaign of speculation and misinformation designed to flesh out the best offers. The Boss sought to move the club to Manhattan, or maybe it was New Jersey, or perhaps he just wanted to create the appearance that all his options were open to jack up the franchise's value in the midst of negotiations to sell. Meanwhile, [Mayor Rudy Giuliani] supported Steinbrenner's explorations, warned the governor of New Jersey to keep her hands off his teams, and battled his rival, Peter Vallone, the head of the city council and author of a ballot referendum that would allow the voters to forbid the use of public funds to facilitate the Boss' move from the Bronx to Manhattan along the Hudson. City taxpayers did not want to hand hundreds of millions to a billionaire, and Vallone's initiative unleashed a rare wave of populist sentiment in New York City.

In 1998, only hours before the fourth home game of the season, a quarter-ton expansion joint crashed through a seat in the loge section along the third-base line. Steinbrenner seized on the accident to declare that the park's very foundation was crumbling—another argument for a new home. However, Gaston Silva, the city's chief buildings investigator, did a full stadium inspection and declared that it could stand for another 75 years. " 'Crumbling' is a popular word teams use when they want a new stadium," says DeMause.

THE PROPOSED NEW STADIUM—BOONDOGGLE, INSULT, OR NECESSARY CIVIC IMPROVEMENT?

Public opposition to a parasitic taxpayer-funded giveaway didn't deter King George. His incestuous ties with the Giuliani administration netted him a new, $70 million minor-league park in Staten Island (the only right-wing borough in the city), the funds for which might've gone toward, say, repairing public schools.

Undeterred by a change at Gracie Mansion and exploiting a loophole in the city's political system that enables the rich and powerful to end-run around a public referendum, Steinbrenner greased enough palms at City Hall to unveil yet another new stadium plan.

Early last year, it was reported that the Yankees would build a new, $750 million stadium across the street from their current home. *New York Business* said that the team would ask for $450 million in public-infrastructure investment to build a hotel and conference center, improve and increase public transportation to the area, and build three new parks elsewhere in the Bronx. They would likely seek to finance the facility by issuing tax-exempt Industrial Development Authority bonds, to be paid off with revenue from the new stadium, which would include

50 megabucks-generating skyboxes. (They could also sell the naming rights for $10 million or so. In other words, the new Stadium could be the House that Wal-Mart Built. Or Yanks Depot.)

GEORGE'S ULTIMATE SCAM

Just when you thought that FrankenStein had emptied his bag of dirty tricks, he has now apparently concocted a brazen scheme in which not only would city taxpayers help subsidize his latest pleasure dome, but so would his fellow baseball owners. Neil DeMause says that the Yankee arch-fiend has uncovered a flaw in the Collective Bargaining Agreement that would force baseball's other 29 teams to pay nearly half its cost.

DeMause described the breathtaking con on the Baseball Prospectus website:

> The Yankees are offering to pay the entire $750 million cost of building a stadium in Macombs Dam Park, across 161st Street from Yankee Stadium. The existing ballpark would be demolished to make way for a parking garage (though the *New York Times* has reported that the design would retain "the ball field

and the most recognizable elements of the structure," which is hard to picture). The city and state would kick in somewhere between $300 million and $450 million to build a new hotel and conference center, and obtain new parkland elsewhere in the Bronx to make up for the destruction of Macombs Dam Park.

DeMause says that the team would foot the bill for the new stadium by exploiting an obscure clause in MLB's Basic Agreement that allows teams to deduct "Stadium Operations Expenses"—including *stadium construction debt*—from their revenue-sharing payments. The Yankees currently pay a marginal revenue-sharing rate of about 39 percent of local revenue, so "taking a deduction for $40 million a year in stadium bond payments would thus earn the Yankees a $15.6 million-a-year write-off on their annual revenue-sharing obligations. Over time, about $300 million of the House That George Built would be paid for by the other 29 teams." Not only that, but any revenue that Steinbrenner gets from the publicly funded hotel and conference center would be pure profit, untouchable by his fellow owners.

In other words, the new ballpark would be less a venue

for baseball games than a tax-sheltering entertainment complex. The new economic paradigm—which could be changed in 2006 when the players and owners revisit the Basic Agreement—encourages teams to pursue non-baseball-related product. A roller coaster going through center field? Anything's possible. (Besides, could it hurt the Yanks' defense any more than Williams and Lofton?)

NOTES

1. Interview with the author.
2. Online chat with Cramer, October 25, 2000, www.cnn.com/COMMUNITY/transcripts/2000/10/25/cramer.
3. *Joe DiMaggio: The Hero's Life*, Richard Ben Cramer (Simon & Schuster, 2000).
4. From www.wordiq.com/definition/New_York_Yankees.

Chapter Seven

YANKEE LOWLIGHTS

Yankee Haters, you have seen the team highlight reel so often, you probably remember Tino's homer off Byung-Hyun Kim in the 2001 Series with more clarity than your own honeymoon. To restore your sanity, I'm performing an intervention. The idea is to replace your bad memories of exultant Yankee victories with deeply satisfying, meaningful reflections. . . . I'm talking about Maz in '61, Edgar driving in Griffey in '95, and Ortiz and Schilling driving a stake through the Bambino's heart last October. In other words, here are 100 years of Yankee Lowlights, the worst moments in franchise history:

1980 ALCS VS. KANSAS CITY ROYALS, GAME 3: BRETT ROASTS THE GOOSE.

1. October 10, 1980. With the Yanks down two games to none in the best-of-five series, they held a 2–1 lead going into the top of the seventh with their ace reliever, Goose Gossage, on the mound. But all-time Yankee nemesis George Brett belted a three-run homer off Gossage—his second homer of the series—and sent the Yankees home. Michael Vogel, writing on Alex Belth's blog, Bronx Banter, said, "I was at that game and don't recall the energy of Yankee Stadium ever deflating so much so quickly."

2002 DIVISION SERIES VS. ANAHEIM ANGELS: THUNDERSTIX

2. In this series, the Halos bombarded Yankee pitching, torpedoing everything close to a strike. Game 2: Back-to-back shots by Garret Anderson and Troy Glaus in the top of the eighth put Anaheim ahead and stunned Yankee fans.

The Angels scored two more and took a 7–4 lead. In the bottom of the inning, the Yanks got one back and loaded the bases with two outs with Mr. November, Derek Jeter, facing Troy Percival. Jeter was called out on a pitch a half-foot outside.

Game 3: An early 6–1 Yankee lead evaporated, Mike Mussina pulled a groin muscle and had to leave the game, and a pair of bloop RBI singles by the Angels in the sixth and seventh tied the game before Bengie Molina's single and Tim Salmon's two-run eighth-inning homer helped Anaheim pull away.

Game 4: The baseball gods continued to curse the Bombers, steering sure home runs foul or keeping them in the park. Jeter was robbed of an extra-base hit by Anderson's incredible catch in left. As 50,000 Anaheim fans rattled their Thunderstix, the Angels mercilessly slew David Wells and ended the Yanks' season with a 10-hit, 8-run bottom of the fifth.

1995 DIVISION SERIES VS. SEATTLE MARINERS: EDGAR THE YANKEE KILLER

3. Game 4: In the Yanks' first playoff appearance in 14 years, they held a 2–1 game lead. But the immobile but

deadly Edgar Martinez went yard twice, one of them a grand slam, as Seattle overcame a 6–1 Yankee lead to tie the series.

Game 5: Donnie Baseball's last game. In the top of the eleventh, a base hit by Randy Velarde—ex-pilot of the Columbus Shuttle—off a relieving Randy Johnson gave the Yanks a one-run lead. But with men on first and second in the bottom of the inning, Edgar played executioner for the second night in a row as he ripped a Jack McDowell pitch down the left-field line and Griffey dashed home from first with the winning run. To relieve their despair, some Yankee fans went out and beat up some Red Sox fans.

1997 DIVISION SERIES VS. CLEVELAND INDIANS, GAME 4: MO BLOWS IT, PART I

4. The Yanks were four outs away from ending the series when, in the bottom of the eighth, their newly anointed closer Mariano Rivera came in to preserve a 2–1 lead. But Sandy Alomar took Rivera's outside fastball over the right-field wall to tie the game. In the ninth with future Yankee malcontent Kenny Lofton on second and two outs, Omar Vizquel hit a ground ball back to Ramiro Mendoza that deflected off his glove and toward the shortstop hole vacated by Jeter, who had expected the ball to go up the middle. Lofton scored the winning run, and the next night the Indians sent the Yanks home to whine away the off-season.

2001 WORLD SERIES VS. ARIZONA DIAMONDBACKS, GAME 7: MO BLOWS IT, PART II

5. In one of the most melodramatic series of all time, the Yanks' two incredible ninth-inning comebacks in Games 5 and 6 seemed to inject their fans with a sense of karmic certitude. In the eighth inning of Game 7, Alfonso Soriano golfed a shoe-top splitter from Curt Schilling deep into the left-center-field seats to put the Yanks up, 2–1. But in the bottom of the ninth, Rivera, who had shut down the Snakes in the eighth, fell apart. After Mark Grace singled to lead off, Rivera threw errantly high to second on Damian Miller's bunt. Jay Bell then bunted right to Rivera, who tossed it to Scott Brosius for the force at third. With plenty of time to get Bell at first for the double play, Brosius, one of the "clutch" Yankees, inexplicably froze and held the ball. Tony Womack's double tied it, and Rivera plunked Craig Counsell to load the bases. Then Luis Gonzalez blooped a single over a questionably drawn-in infield

to end the series. The Yanks and their fans—who after 9/11 had apparently felt that it was Arizona's patriotic duty to lose the series—were in toxic shock. It was if the terrorists had won.

JUNE 12, 2003, YANKEE STADIUM, INTERLEAGUE GAME VS. HOUSTON ASTROS: STEP RIGHT UP AND NO-HIT THE YANKS

6. Six Astro pitchers combined to pitch the first no-hitter against the Yanks since Hoyt Wilhelm's in 1958. At one point, eight straight Yanks struck out, a team record. After ace Roy Oswalt pulled a groin muscle in the second inning, Peter Munro, Kirk Saarloos, Brad Lidge, Octavio Dotel, and Billy Wagner finished off the 8–0 win. It was the most pitchers ever used to complete a no-hitter, and the Yanks swung so feebly that the Astros could've brought in J. R. Richard and Larry Dierker without changing the result. After the game, Joe Torre admitted, "This is one of the worst games I've ever been involved in. It was a total, inexcusable performance." It was rumored that Steinbrenner kept the team for extra batting practice until 5 a.m.—with the Stadium lights turned off.

1960 WORLD SERIES VS. PITTSBURGH PIRATES:
MAZ'S WALK-OFF

7. A series in which the heavily-favored Yanks outscored the Pirates 55–27, beating them 16–3, 12–0, and 10–0, and yet lost the series. In Game 7 at Pittsburgh's cavernous Forbes Field, the Yanks led 7–4 going into the bottom of the eighth, when the Pirates rallied for five runs, which included a three-run blast by catcher Hal Smith. (This led broadcaster Jack Brickhouse to say that "Forbes Field at this moment is an outdoor insane asylum.") Behind 9–7, the Yankees came back with two runs in the top of the ninth to tie the score. In the bottom of the ninth, light-hitting second baseman Bill Mazeroski, who had hit only 11 home runs during the season, led off against Ralph Terry. On a 1–0 count, Maz lined a ball over the left-field wall as left fielder Yogi Berra turned his back to home plate and, like a character in Beckett, waited despondently for a ball to come back in play that never would. Red Smith described the moment in his column the following day: "Terry watched the ball disappear, brandished his glove hand high overhead, shook himself like a wet spaniel, and started fighting through the mobs that came boiling from the stands to use Mazeroski like a trampoline."

In the succeeding years, the halt and the lame would make pilgrimages to Pittsburgh, just to touch some of Mazeroski's Big League Chew.

1955 WORLD SERIES VS. BROOKLYN DODGERS: DEM BUMS SHOW YANKS WHO'S BOSS

8. The Dodgers, who had lost to the Yanks in the Series in 1947, 1949, 1952, and 1953, were down two games to none and confronting another "next year," but 23-year-old lefty Johnny Podres beat the Bombers 8–3 in the third game and shut them out 2–0 in Game 7 in front of a crowd of 62,465. Sandy Amoros, sent in as a defensive replacement by Dodgers manager Walter Alston in the sixth inning, immediately saved the lead and the series. With two men on, he sprinted from left-center to the left-field foul line to nab Yogi Berra's wrong-field fly, then started a relay that doubled up Billy Martin off first.

1981 WORLD SERIES VS. LOS ANGELES DODGERS: FRAZIER NEEDS A SHRINK

9. Bad managing by Bob Lemon—in Game 6, he pinch-hit for his best pitcher, Tommy John, in the bottom of the fourth inning—and atrocious relief pitching from George

Frazier (brought in for John), who set a Series record with three losses, lifted the Dodgers from a 2–0 game deficit, as they took four straight. Afterward, Steinbrenner issued a public apology to Yankee fans, then "rendered" Frazier to a Middle Eastern country where torture is legal.

1964 WORLD SERIES VS. ST. LOUIS CARDINALS, GAME 7: GIBSON DRIVES A STAKE INTO THE DYNASTY

10. Bob Gibson held on to an early 7–0 lead and beat the Yanks, 7–5, to clinch the series for St. Louis. It was the last Fall Classic for veterans Mickey Mantle, Whitey Ford, Bobby Richardson, Tony Kubek, and Clete Boyer, and the team wouldn't appear again in October for 12 years.

CHOKING UP: THE WORST COLLAPSE SINCE THE 1929 MARKET

Around midnight on October 21, 2004, everything changed. The sun revolved around the earth. Time ticked backward. The Babe stayed in Beantown, Yaz hit a walk-off against the Goose, Buckner caught Mookie's grounder, and Pesky nailed Slaughter at the plate. Red Sox Nation was triumphant, and the result was Yankee *Götterdämmerung*, the twilight of the Bronx idols. After the Yanks had become the first team in baseball history to blow a 3–0 lead in a post-season series, one stunned fan blurted, "Everything I've always known to be right has been proven wrong."

Little did anyone know that Mariano Rivera's walk of Kevin Millar in the ninth inning of Game 4 would lead to a cataclysm whose repercussions for the Yankee franchise might be felt for a decade or more.

Among the incredulous faithful and the fickle media, the postmortems for the team's mind-boggling, four-game ALCS choke—called by one writer "the lowest moment in the organization's history"—began immediately. The Yankee hitters, who had pummeled Boston pitching in Games 1 and 3 of the series, suddenly developed corked heads, eschewing their trademark patience and swinging wildly, even while ahead in the count. They did this not just against a one-legged Curt Schilling, but against Derek Lowe, who'd had such a deplorable season he'd been relegated to long relief before the playoffs began. In Game 7, the Yanks Millionaires' Row could only manage one hit in six innings against Lowe, who was pitching on two days' rest.

The starting pitchers, outside of Mike Mussina and Jon Lieber in Game 2, were pounded by Papi David Ortiz and his *niños*—especially Kevin Brown, who Yankee fans wished had broken his right hand instead of his left. And Tom Gordon and Mo Rivera were human defibrillators, coughing up late-inning leads in Games 4 and 5 to bring the unconscious Sox back to life.

Joe Torre managed on autopilot, and without Don Zimmer to jog his memory, forgot that Kenny Lofton was even on the team. A fool's parade of Brian Cashman's acquisitions—Brown, Javier Vásquez, Esteban Loaiza, Félix Heredia—took turns throwing batting practice to the Red Sox.

Steinbrenner's "warriors" turned out to be matchstick soldiers—especially golden boy Alex Rodriguez, who not only dematerialized at the plate, but whose petulant, bush-league swipe at Bronson Arroyo while running out an infield tapper in the eighth inning of Game 6 was a cringe-inducing cry for help. Mr. November, Derek Jeter, hit .200 in the series, made two errors, and displayed about as much lateral movement as an armored personnel carrier—and then told the press that "this isn't the same [Dynasty] team." Across the entire organization there was a total absence of accountability—the Bush Administration in jockstraps. Gary Sheffield foolishly taunted the Red Sox after Game 3 (saying they weren't winners), words that the Boston team used as motivational fuel. Then he pretty much went 0—for the rest of the series.

In the end, the Yanks came up short—in pitching, hitting, fielding, roster construction, and guts. The Sox completed this humiliation by drubbing the St. Louis Cardinals in four straight.

The Evil Empire has finally fallen. What will replace it? And how will the Emperor respond? Will he unleash pepper spray on his front office? Kidnap Randy Johnson? Sell Joe Torre's identity to a Nigerian gang? All we know is that during the off-season, an overbearing owner, a phlegmatic manager, a beleaguered GM, and a variety of executive lackeys will be locked in mortal combat in a Florida office. Call it "Tampa Survivor."

The All-Time Worst Yankee Teams

The Barren Years I: The Highlanders

The Highlanders are the batty old uncle in the Yankee attic, the part of themselves they dare not mention in public, lest their mythology be darkened. Outside of two second-place finishes (1904, 1910), they spent their 17 years of existence skulking around in the American League cellar. They played in Hilltop Park (for which they were named) in Washington Heights, in Manhattan, until 1913, when they moved to become tenants of the New York Giants in the Polo Grounds. At this point, perhaps influenced by a local sportswriter, Mark Roth, who had already dubbed them in print, they changed their name to the Yankees. It was only in 1921, when the Giants, threatened by Ruth's notoriety and the Yankees' higher attendance, evicted them from the Polo Grounds, that the team hatched its plan for what would become Yankee Stadium.

The Barren Years II:
CBS Launches a Bomb

Even though the Yanks had won the AL pennant in 1964, owner Dan Topping executed two epochal moves he'd planned during the season: (1) to fire manager Yogi Berra, who he blamed for the team's disappointing early-season showing and World Series loss to the Cardinals, and (2) to sell the team to CBS. Following the World Series, the network purchased 80 percent of the Yanks for $11.2 million. (They bought the rest later.)

Their investment fell apart on

them as the Yankees, under manager Johnny Keane (the Cardinals skipper in '64), had their first losing season since 1925. Thus began the "Horace Clarke era" and a descent to the cellar so precipitous, it was as if somebody had opened an enormous trapdoor under Yankee Stadium. The team's last-place finish had many causes: Tony Kubek and Whitey Ford had retired, Roger Maris had lost most of his power, Mantle was breaking down physically, and their farm system was barren. Players such as Jerry Kenny, Ross Moschitto, and Steve Whitaker impersonated Yankees and indelibly imprinted themselves on the formative minds of the next generation of Yankee fans, and would cost them years of therapy as grown-ups.

So embarrassing are the years 1965–71 that the biggest highlight from that era in the team's media guide is the painting of Yankee Stadium.

The Barren Years III:
Meet the New Boss...

The Yankees in the 1980s were the victim of Bad George, the evil-twin owner who overhauled the roster like a cracked-up fashion designer perpetually searching for a new "look." From 1982 to 1991 the team was a revolving door of managers (11 changes) and players. Billy Martin was hired and fired six times, and the team more resembled a bad comedy pilot than the most successful franchise in sports. Yet for most of the '80s, the team was a contender, and it was only late in the decade that they crashed.

The last-place 1990 team reached the nadir of Yankee history. It had the next-to-worst pitching in the league. (When Timothy Leary is your best pitcher, it's time to take some LSD.) And the hitters were even worse. Jesse Barfield batted .246 and struck out 150 times. Roberto Kelly, who was impossible to walk, struck out 148 times. The full-time catcher was Bob Geren, who batted .213. There were more cancers in the clubhouse than at Sloane-Kettering.

NOTES

All historical material in this chapter is taken from baseball library.com, baseballreference.com, and various series wrap-ups from ESPN.com and other sources.

Chapter Eight

THE ALL-TIME
WORST YANKEES

L adies and gentlemen, here are your New York Yankees:

Omar Moreno	CF
Dave Collins	RF
Oscar Azocar	LF
Johnny Sturm	1B
Carlos May	DH
Jake Gibbs	C

Celerino Sánchez   3B

Alvaro Espinoza   SS

Horace Clarke   2B

Starting pitchers: Andy Hawkins, Ed Whitson, Jeff Weaver, Mike "Swapping Partners" Kekich

Relievers: Dale Murray, Félix Heredia

Bench: Tuck Stainback (OF), Red Kleinow (C), "Chicken" Hawks (1B), Sandy Alomar, Jr. (2B), Jim Mason (SS)

Manager: Stump Merrill

I know what you're thinking: "Those are Yankees? I must've fallen through a wormhole in time-space to an alternate universe where the mighty Bombers whiff, stumble, and throw nothing but gopher balls, a universe ruled by Dick Radatz. Right?"

Well, no. These players actually existed and were carefully chosen after much perusal of the historical record: They're the all-time worst players to have worn the pinstripes. Call them the anti-Yanks.

I chose them based on the following criteria: (1) they

had to have completed a full season or so with the Yankees; (2) they had to really suck, especially at the plate.

Here's the scouting report:

CATCHER: JAKE GIBBS 1965–1971

Anybody who followed the Yankees in the 1960s remembers Gibbs, who was always described by Yankee announcers as a "good-looking ex-quarterback from Ol' Miss." It was generally acknowledged that the former All-American couldn't hit but provided solid defense. But in his three seasons between Elston Howard and Thurman Munson in which he filled the catcher's spot, he had a below-average fielding percentage and range factor. In 1967, Gibbs made a whopping 16 errors in 99 games. Perhaps this was because he'd been a third baseman in college, which makes you wonder why the Yanks tried to convert him.

His 10-year-career batting line:

HR 25 RBI 146 BB 120 K 231 BA .233 OBP .289 SLG .321

BACKUP: RED KLEINOW 1904–1910

In 1904, the New York Highlanders were tied with the Red Sox in a game that would decide the American League pennant (which would've been New York's first). Then 41-game-winner Jack Chesbro sailed a spitball over Kleinow's head, which allowed the winning run to score. It was ruled a wild pitch, but Kleinow took heat for failing to catch it. It would be another 17 years before the franchise won a pennant. At the plate, Kleinow sucked in an era when "sucking" was known only to French people: His career OPS was .551, almost 100 points lower than the league's.

FIRST BASE: JOHNNY STURM 1941

He was the starting first baseman for the 1941 World Championship team and was credited by many with alerting the Yankees to a young prospect named Mickey Mantle. Yet it's hard to believe that any team—even one with Joe DiMaggio—could win a pennant with a first baseman who hit .239 with three home runs and 36 RBI in 124 games, and who wasn't that great with the glove, either. Sturm mangled his hand in a wartime accident, but it's hard to believe he could've played much worse even with it healthy.

BACKUP: NELSON "CHICKEN" HAWKS 1921

Don't laugh yet; the man did play with Babe Ruth, in 1921, when he had one home run and 22 RBI.

SECOND BASE: HORACE CLARKE 1965–1974

The poster child for the sad-sack post-dynastic-collapse Yankees of the mid-'6os, Clarke—with his goggle-sized glasses, wispy physique and fey cricketeer swing—appears regularly in the nightmares of Yankee fans. Even in an era when middle infielders were typecast as good-glove, no-hit, it's amazing that the Bronx Bombers could've let such an offensive black hole remain the starting second baseman for nine years. (OPS .621 League OPS .685) Due credit: "Hoss" was an above-average fielder, as was his backup on the All-Yankees-Suck squad, Sandy Alomar, Sr.

SHORTSTOP: ALVARO ESPINOZA 1989–1991

Another good fielder—he had a far superior range factor—Espy was another ghost at the plate. In three more or less full seasons, he had seven home runs and 94 RBI. His only skill with a bat in his hand was novelty hitting, as he was one of only four players in history to knock a fair ball that got stuck in a stadium obstruction—when his drive lodged in an overhead speaker at the Metrodome.

BACKUP: JIM MASON

Mason had the lowest batting average in the 1970s of any player with at least 1,500 at-bats. He hit below .200 in six of his eight seasons (not counting his nine at-bats in 1971), with a career high of .250 in 1974, his only year as a regular. And yet, in the 1976 World Series, after he replaced Fred Stanley in Game 3, he hit a solo homer in the seventh inning, the only man in history to hit a homerun in his only lifetime Series at-bat.

THIRD BASE: CELERINO SÁNCHEZ 1972–1973

In two seasons—a little over 250 at-bats—Sánchez hit exactly one home run, had 31 RBI, and walked a grand total of 12 times. He went to the Yanks from the Mexico City Tigers of the Mexican League for Ossie Chavarria in what was more of a prisoner exchange than a trade. Prices of his baseball cards: 35, (1973), $1 (1974).

BACKUP: JOHN KENNEDY

Played third in 1967 as if he'd been assassinated.

LEFT FIELD: OSCAR AZOCAR 1990

Boy, this team is so light-hitting, they're approaching full weightlessness. Azocar had a .612 OPS in his one season in New York, a full 103 points lower than the league average.

BACKUP: TUCK STAINBACK

In parts of three seasons, compiled five home runs, 42 RBI, and 20 walks. Claim to fame: Once traded for Dizzy Dean.

CENTER FIELD: OMAR MORENO 1983–1984

"Omar the Outmaker" was arguably one of the worst hitters in baseball history. Acquired by the team during George's brief infatuation with speed, he struck out often, walked almost never, and chopped at the ball as if it were a greasy pig that had gotten loose on the field. I'd include his lifetime stats here, but I'm firmly against pornography.

RIGHT FIELD: DAVE COLLINS 1982

For the Yanks, the early 1980s were the Dead Ball Era. Collins was a big part of it in 1982, when he hit three home runs, drove in 25 runs, and had a .315 OBP and .330 slugging percentage. Worse than that, a guy brought in for his speed was thrown out in 8 of 21 stolen base attempts.

DH: CARLOS MAY 1976–1977

Carlos, younger brother of Lee May, had some great seasons for the White Sox in the early '70s, even after blowing off his thumb on National Guard duty. But by the time the Yanks got him, he was all thumbs. May was perhaps the only player in baseball history to wear his birth date—May 17—on the back of his uniform.

STARTING PITCHERS:

ED WHITSON 1985

A reviled name among Yankee fans, and a symbol of the small-market star who can't cut it in the Big Apple. Whitson came over as a glamorous free agent, pitched miserably, broke manager Billy Martin's arm in a bar one night after scuffling with a patron, was so unnerved by the demanding Yankee crowds that he threw up before each start, was the target of such abuse that in 1986, manager Lou Piniella wouldn't pitch him at Yankee Stadium, and was virtually booed out of town.

ANDY HAWKINS 1988

His former manager Dick Williams dubbed him the "Timid Texan." (The 1980s Yanks apparently wanted to corner the market in gutlessness.) Best remembered for pitching a no-hitter against the White Sox and *losing 4–0*. In 1990, Hawkins had three starts at Fenway Park, pitched a total of one inning, and gave up 18 runs. That's an ERA of 162.00.

JEFF WEAVER

His 2003 performance in pinstripes was one of the worst by a starter in recent history: In 159 innings, he gave up 211 hits. His 5.99 ERA was more than 1.5 runs worse than the league average. As if his performance wasn't putrid enough, Weaver didn't endear himself to the team with his all-night carousing and obstinate refusal to reconsider his pitching approach. His horrendous 2003 season ended when Joe Torre reverted to his "Clueless Joe" days and brought Weaver into Game 4 of the 2003 Series. Weaver promptly gave up the game-winning homer to ukulele-hitting shortstop Alex Gonzalez, which turned the Series in Florida's favor.

MIKE KEKICH 1969–1972

Hard-throwing lefty who consistently stunk. Ended up pitching in Mexico and Japan. If only Kekich could've swapped careers with, say, Mickey Lolich.

RELIEF PITCHERS:

RIGHTY: DALE MURRAY (SEE "ALL-TIME WORST YANKEE TRADES") 1983–1985

Another former standout (for the Expos), Murray was among the many players—most free agents with declining skills—who treated Yankee Stadium as if it were Leisure Village. He had lost his fastball somewhere between Montreal and Toronto, the latter of whom peddled him to a credulous Steinbrenner in exchange for Fred McGriff.

LEFTY: FÉLIX HEREDIA 2003–2004

A lefty specialist who was battered like an equal-opportunity *piñata*. Heredia's body—a short torso and outsized legs—looks as if it was hastily assembled by a couple of drunken med students. This could've messed up his mechanics and led to his 2004 line: 38.7 innings, 44 hits, 28 runs, 20 walks, 25 strikeouts, 5 home runs, and an ERA of 6.28 (6.39 against lefties!). Heredia's season was interrupted by a demotion to Class A ball, but this wasn't good enough for some Yankee fans, who drafted a "Trade Félix Heredia" petition. It read, "By signing this petition you agree that New York Yankee 'Picher' [sic] Félix (Ball 4)

Heredia needs to be either released or traded to the Red Sox!" It was posted on a website "provided to help concerned citizens rally support for issues they believe in."

MANAGER: CARL "STUMP" MERRILL 1990–1991

One of the many longtime organizational retreads who sacrifice the last vestiges of professional pride to be jacked around by Steinbrenner, Merrill in 1990 presided over only the Yanks' second last-place finish since the Highlanders era. His two-year record: 120 wins, 155 losses, a .436 winning percentage. Since his firing in 1991, Merrill has traveled the globe as a special consultant and was last seen managing an all-Shiite team in Iraq.

MANAGER-IN-WAITING: NORMAN ARTHUR "TABASCO KID" ELBERFELD 1908

A hot-tempered player-manager, The Kid compiled the lowest winning percentage—.276—in Yankees history. He had longevity, though: In 1936, at the age of 61, he pinch-hit for his Fulton Kitty League team and grounded out to third.

Yanks' Biggest
Bonus Baby Busts

In the 40 years that the amateur draft has been in existence, the Yanks have produced only five first-round picks who made an impact in the majors, and only two of those—Thurman Munson and Derek Jeter—contributed to New York. They team has a track record of much-ballyhooed prospects who soon fizzle out: Hensley "Bam-Bam" Meulens, Shea Morentz, David Walling. But there are two who flamed out in especially Hindenburg-like fashion:

BUST #1: Brien Taylor
A fireballing left-hander who could throw in the high 90s, he got a $1 million bonus when he signed as the #1

overall pick in 1991. But in the off-season before his first year in pro ball, Taylor moronically injured his shoulder trying to break up a bar fight involving his brother. (If the Yankees were a Wagnerian opera, the bar fight would be a major leitmotif.) Taylor made innumerable attempts to recover, but the damage to his arm was irreparable.

BUST #2: Drew Henson

Biggest bust in Yankee history. The Yanks gave the multitalented Henson a $2 million bonus after selecting him in the third round in 1998. (He had first-round talent, but he dropped because of concerns that he would choose an NFL career.) When Henson wouldn't commit to baseball full-time, the Yankees traded him to the Reds as part of a package for

Denny Neagle in July 2000. Henson then pulled the old "I'll only play for the Yankees" ploy (previously used by Hideki Irabu), so the Reds dealt him back to New York for outfielder Wily Mo Pena and $1.9 million in 2001. The Yankees gave him a six-year, $17 million contract with the provision that he abandon football. But Steinbrenner prematurely rushed him to the upper levels of the Yankee system. Three years and 358 strikeouts with Columbus later, Henson abandoned baseball to play in the NFL. Meanwhile, Pena tore up the National League in 2004.

NOTE

All historical information and statistics were taken from *Total Baseball* (edited by Pete Palmer and John Thorn, Warner Books, 1989), baseball-reference.com, and baseballlibrary.com.

Chapter Nine

THE YANKEE KILLERS[1]

Yankee Haters everywhere know that sometimes rooting against the Yankees is more gratifying than cheering for their home team. In this war of emotional antagonism, they often have to rely on proxies, third-party players who punish and dominate the Bombers. Here is an all-star team of players who see red when they see the interlocking NY: The Yankee Killers.

C: CARLTON FISK

In his 22-year Hall of Fame career, Fisk hit well against the entire American League, but against the Yankees he added his fists and a pugnacious attitude. In August 1973, in a game tied 2–2 in the top of the ninth, he brawled with Yankee counterpart Thurman Munson after the New York backstop tried to run him over during a missed squeeze bunt by Gene Michael. Boston won the game, 3–2, in the bottom of the inning. Seventeen years later, while with the White Sox, Fisk berated the Yankees' Deion Sanders for not running out a pop-up. While Sanders was too stunned to respond, Pudge's tirade nearly instigated a fracas between the two teams. "Yankee pinstripes, Yankee pride," Fisk scoffed. "I'm playing for the other team, and it offended me." Sanders apologized the next day.

DH: EDGAR MARTINEZ

The 41-year-old Martinez was a designated hit man for Yankee pitching throughout his just-completed 18-year career, batting .323 with 22 homers and 100 RBI in 130 games. Hell, his double in the bottom of the ninth in Game 5 of the 1995 Divisional Series delayed the Dynasty for a full year. But the Yanks shouldn't be embarrassed—Edgar the Great was an equal-opportunity basher, with 309 lifetime home runs, 1,261 RBI, and a .933 OPS average, stats he would've padded if Seattle hadn't buried him in their minor-league system early in his career. Clearly the best DH ever.

1B: DAVID ORTIZ

"Papi" cemented his plaque in the anti-Yankee Hall of Fame by almost single-handedly un-hexing the Red Sox in last year's ALCS. The numbers—OBP: .533 (with 12 walks), SLG: .813—don't even tell the whole story, as he had two game-winning hits, and his five homers all came at crucial times. His home run ended the Yankees' sweep dream in Game 4 of the ALCS, and his blast off Tom Gordon signaled a comeback in Game 5, which Ortiz also ended, with a 14th-inning single. In Game 7, seconds after Johnny Damon was cut down at the plate in the first inning, Ortiz dispatched Mystique and Aura to the Retired Strippers Home with his two-run blast off Kevin Brown. The rout was on.

2B: DICK McAULIFFE

The guy with perhaps the most awkward batting stance in major-league history—leaning back toward the catcher, bat held high over his head, facing almost square to the pitcher, then raising his front leg high—was also a forerunner of today's slugging middle infielders, one of the few such creatures in 1960s baseball. And boy, did he feast on Yankee blood. In his 15-year career, he had 24 HRs and 67 RBI versus New York, personal bests against any one team.

SS: SCOTT FLETCHER

During a 15-year career as an infielder and DH with the Rangers, White Sox, and other clubs, Fletcher played for six teams and hit .262. But against the Yankees, journeyman Fletcher turned into Honus Wagner: He hit .335 against New York before retiring in 1995.

3B: GEORGE BRETT

Hall-of-Famer Brett hit .358 in four postseason series against the Yanks, three of which—the 1976, 1977, and 1978 ALCS—they won, despite Brett's heroics. In the third game of the 1978 ALCS, he hit three home runs against Catfish Hunter only to watch Doug Bird give up a game-winning home run to Thurman Munson. Brett finally gave the Yanks their comeuppance in 1980, when his three-run homer off Goose Gossage in Game 3 put the Royals in the World Series for the first time.

OF: KEN GRIFFEY, JR.

Griffey always explained his career performance against the Yankees—.312 average, 33 home runs, and 92 RBI in 447 at-bats—as a kind of revenge killing. It seems that when Griffey's dad, Ken Griffey, Sr., played for the Yanks in the early 1980s, Billy Martin kicked Junior out of the clubhouse because the child was too boisterous.

OF: CARL YASTRZEMSKI

In his Hall of Fame career, the great Yaz compiled 45 home runs and 145 RBI—an MVP-caliber season—against the Yankees alone. Most Sox fans remember with painful clarity his game-ending pop-up against Goose Gossage in the 1978 one-game playoff, while forgetting that he tagged Cy Young winner Ron Guidry for a home run earlier in that contest.

OF: TONY OLIVA

Oliva was one of the most graceful yet punishing hitters of the mid-1960s and would certainly have reached the baseball pantheon if he hadn't suffered a debilitating knee injury. Still, he was a three-time batting champion and a lifetime .304 hitter (over 14 seasons). Against the Yankees, though, he took his game into the stratosphere, slugging .527 (very high for his pitching-dominant era) with 28 homers, more than he hit against any other club.

LHP: BILL LEE

Although the Spaceman went 12–5 against the Yankees while with the Red Sox, the always-candid Lee has admitted that his record was built mostly against substandard Yankee clubs of the early 1970s and that he benefited from the old Yankee Stadium's yawning left field. But mostly, he says, it's because pitchers are smarter than hitters. "Hitters are Neanderthals," Lee says. "Pitchers are smarter than hitters—except for Roger Clemens."

RHP: FRANK LARY

The original "Yankee Killer" (as he was dubbed by the press), Frank Lary was an average pitcher on a mediocre Detroit team in the 1950s, but he somehow morphed into a Power Ranger whenever facing the Yankees. How else to explain his anomalous 12-year career? Lifetime overall record: 128–116; record against the Yanks: 28–13, including 7–1 in 1958, when the Tigers were 77–77 and finished 15 games behind the first-place Bombers. (He went 9–14 against the rest of the AL that year.)

RHP: WALTER JOHNSON

The Big Train had the Yanks tied to his tracks: He notched 60 of his 417 wins against the Yankees—the most by any opposing pitcher. What makes Johnson's record remarkable is that he won all those games while playing for the Washington Senators, a perennial AL bottom-dweller. In 1908, Johnson pitched three shutouts in four days against the Yankees, then known as the Highlanders. In 1923, he gave New York its first defeat at their new park, Yankee Stadium, before 70,000 fans. In 1924, with his career winding down, Johnson led the Senators, picked to finish seventh, to the pennant, just ahead of New York.

RHP: CURT SCHILLING

It could be said that he's the undoer of curses, the antidote to Yankee mojo. First he stopped the Dynasty in its tracks in Game 1 of the 2001 Series, allowing only one run and three hits, striking out eight and walking one. His Series totals were 21.3 innings, 12 hits, four earned runs, 26 strike-outs, and two walks.

In Game 6 of the 2004 ALCS, on a torn tendon in his ankle that led to the bleeding socks—the stigmata to Red Sox fans—Schill shut the Yanks down on one run and four hits, and drove a stake into their black hearts.

MANAGER: AL LOPEZ

"El Señor," as he was known, managed the only two non-Yankee American League teams to win pennants during New York's 1949–1964 mega-dynasty. In 1954, his Cleveland Indians won a league-record 111 games, finishing eight games ahead of the Yanks (who, ironically, compiled their highest single-season win total during that 15-year run). And five years later, Lopez did it again, with his "Go-Go" Chicago White Sox.

COACH: FRAN PIROZZOLO

Even minor coaches—ones so low on the totem pole they don't even wear uniforms—can kill Yankees. Take Fran Pirozzolo,[2] a "mental skills coach" who worked for the Yankees from 1996 to 2002, then turned Benedict Arnold and helped the Marlins' Josh Beckett and Pudge Rodriguez prepare for the 2003 World Series. As George King wrote in the New York *Post*, "Pirozzolo continued to hurt the Yankees this past October when he worked closely with Red Sox ace Curt Schilling, communicating with the self-centered Schilling on a daily basis" through the postseason. Pirozzolo propounds a program called "guided visual imagery," which is something Schilling heavily endorses. Kings wrote that Pirozzolo helped Schilling handle the trade to Boston and persuaded him to log on to the Sons of Sam Horn Red Sox site and tell their fans that he was there to break The Curse. Now if he can only get Schilling to visualize keeping his mouth shut.

NOTES

1. Material from this chapter is taken from a story by Bill O'Keefe in the New York *Daily News*, July 2003, Retrosheet.org, baseballlibrary.com, and Richard Lally (in an e-mail interview with the author, September 2004).

2. George King, New York *Post*, November 3, 2004.

Chapter Ten

THE DYNASTY

S ure, they were the "consummate pros" who pulled more October Surprises than the Bush family. But who among us wants to relive the Yankee Dynasty? (For self-flagellation, we always have the YES Network.) No, it already haunts our dreams, waking and sleeping— and besides, it didn't *have* to happen. Consider:

✦ What if George Steinbrenner wasn't suspended by Fay Vincent for his involvement with Howard Spira?

Then maybe Gene Michael wouldn't have gotten a free hand to draft the Yankee nucleus, hire Buck Showalter, and rebuild the team.

AND:

✦ What if Michael failed to dissuade Steinbrenner from trading the young, struggling Bernie Williams and Mariano Rivera (which the owner came very close to doing)?

AND:

✦ What if Jeffrey Maier's dad restrained him from putting his glove over the right-field fence in the eighth inning of Game 1 of the 1996 ALCS and Tony Tarasco caught Jeter's game-tying homer?

AND:

✦ What if umpire Carlos Hernandez correctly called Mark Langston's 2–2 right-down-the-middle pitch to Tino Martinez a strike in the seventh inning of Game 1 of the 1998 World Series, with the score tied 5–5? Maybe the Pods take the game and—who knows?— the title.

You get the picture. All that followed—the pennants, parades, new mutant species of front-running Yankee fans that haunt our dreams, awake and asleep—might never have happened if not for the worm of fate.

But it all did happen. And we'll face it with dignity, like men, by taking potshots at some of the Dynasty's most iconic members:

SIX REASONS WHY DEREK JETER SUCKS

1. *He's totally overrated.* In the "Holy Trinity" of AL shortstops, he's Curly. Except for 1999, he's been completely trounced offensively by Nomah and A-Rod, with far less power than either. In almost the exact same number of at-bats, A-Rod has 381 home runs and 1,095 RBI, to Jeter's 150 homers and 593 RBI. Nomar has 182 homers and 710 RBI in *almost a thousand fewer at-bats than Jeter.* A-Rod regularly has posted OPS averages 100 to 150 points higher than Jeter's. Lifetime, A-Rod has a .955 OPS and Nomar a .919, to Jeter's .848. Jeter's defense had become so putrid that even his hitherto-unquestioning supporters in the New York media were urging him to switch places with A-Rod or take a hike to the outfield. (To be fair, his defensive stats, such as range factor, improved to slightly above average in 2004—and he won a disputed Gold Glove award—but most likely that was due to A-Rod's exceptional range at third, which allowed Jeter to shade to his left, or weaker, side.)

2. *Celebrity nooky.* Mariah Carey, Vanessa Minnillo, Jessica Alba, Anna Kournikova. The life cycle of the teen female heartthrob is instant stardom, mass adulation, screwing Derek Jeter, and doing infomercials by age 25.

3. *PR face for sweatshop-labor-exploiting multinational.* Among Jeter's endorsement deals is one with Nike's Team Jordan, the division that carries His Unfairness's name and logo. Jetes even has a signature training shoe, the Nike Jumpman Jet, that ghetto youth are most assuredly shooting each other over.

4. *Hypocrite.* Affects a bland, above-the-fray persona mistaken for "class," while (according to intimates quoted in "Jeter–A-Rod feud" stories) privately bearing grudges more unforgivingly than a Sicilian don.

5. *Boring.* Like most athletes, says almost nothing that even hints at personality.

6. *Scapegoats teammates for his poor performance.* After last year's ALCS, he blurted to reporters that "This isn't the same team" as the Dynasty club. Jeter hit .200 and made two errors.

WHY CHUCKIE CAN'T THROW

Someday, psychiatrists consulting the DSM-IV will find in its pages, along with generalized anxiety disorder and schizophrenia, something called Knoblauch's Syndrome. Its primary symptom is the sudden inability to accurately throw a baseball from second base to first, and it was named after the Yankee second baseman, who went from adidas All-Star to Rawlings basket case within a year after the Yanks acquired him from Minnesota.

Midway through the 1998 season, the former Gold Glover suddenly developed a mental tic—Joe Torre gave it the scientific term "the yips"—that caused him to hesitate after fielding the ball, then make throws that landed in the first-base boxes. It was like a remake of *Pride of the Yankees* written by the staff of *The Simpsons*.

Unlike Steve Sax, who, 15 years earlier, suffered a similar problem but who conquered it within one season, Knobby never did. He had a league-leading 26 errors in 1999—14 of them on souvenir tosses. By June 28 of 2000, he had made 15 more, most on throws. Finally Torre moved him to left field during spring training of 2001, where he both fielded badly and lost his hitting ability as well. After the Yanks let him go, he played left field for Kansas City for a year, then retired.

COULD SAINT JOE BE A HACK, AFTER ALL?

In 1996, almost overnight, Joe Torre went from "Clueless Joe" to omniscient seer, a leader whose wise counsel and quiet strength led a squadron of "warriors" to a World Championship. Yet, in 15 years of prior managerial experience, for the Mets, Braves, and Cardinals, he'd won only one division title and was a cumulative 109 games under .500. And given an All-Star team virtually every year since 2001, he has failed to win a World Series. Moreover, his once-sure touch seems to have deserted him. In the twelfth inning of Game 4 of the 2003 Series against the Florida Marlins, with Mariano Rivera sitting in the bullpen and to the incredulity of Yankee fans, he brought Jeff Weaver into a game tied 3–3. The sullen Weaver promptly served up the game-winning home run to punchless shortstop Alex Gonzalez, and it turned the Series around. In the 2004 league-championship series, his team blew a 3–0 lead to the Red Sox as Torre managed as if George had a .45 to his head, treating almost everybody in his bullpen except Rivera and (bizarrely) Tanyon Sturtze as if they might try to pick his pocket during a pitching change. He made Kenny Lofton more invisible than if he'd been a guest host on the *Chevy Chase Show*, when Lofton's pinch-running speed may have led to a Yankee victory in Game 5. Every year, Torre's gone out of his way to assemble a Bench of the Living Dead, which means the Yankees go into the post-season with a four- to-five-man handicap. More and more, it's looking as if the dynasty was more a case of Torre being handed a team of exceptional players and staying out of their way.

No, Saint Joe isn't the genius he's cracked up to be. After all, what does it say about your intelligence when your "brain" is Don Zimmer?

CONEY

When he arrived in the Bronx and became enshrined for his admittedly gutsy performances and his perfect game, "hired gun" David Cone (so labeled for his mercenary club-jumping) brought with him enough baggage to have his own carousel. As a New York Met, he was linked to a rape scandal involving teammates Daryl Boston, Vince

Coleman, and Dwight Gooden. Although he was never under investigation, the incident was the second time in five months that a rape charge had surfaced with his name attached. In September 1991, a woman accused Cone of raping her in a Philadelphia hotel room the night before his 19-strikeout game, but police found no basis for the charge.

Also around that time, three women filed a sexual harassment lawsuit against the right-hander, claiming that he exposed himself to them while he was in the bullpen during a 1989 game at Shea Stadium. After becoming a Yankee, Coney seemed to reform, but his reputation as a man of "character" in the clubhouse was built on many years of massaging the New York beat writers with colorful quotes that reeked of manufactured sincerity.

TIM RAINES

During his prime years starring for the Montreal Expos in the 1980s, Raines admitted he was a cocaine junkie who would keep a vial of blow in his pocket and slide headfirst to protect the vial's contents. They didn't call him "Rock" for nothing.

WADE BOGGS

What will appear on his Hall of Fame plaque:

+ 5-time batting champion
+ 2-time All-Star
+ 3,010 career hits

What *should* appear on his Hall of Fame plaque:

+ Sued by a flight attendant for threatening to "kick [her] fat lips in" after she allegedly refused to serve him a final beer before landing.
+ Sued for $12 million by former mistress Margo Adams for breach of oral contract (palimony). Settled out of court.
+ Admitted to being a sex addict on national TV.
+ Was run over by his wife. When authorities arrived, Boggs claimed that he fell out of the car and she rolled over him without noticing.

JOSÉ CANSECO

Yes, he, too, was a Yankee—at least for 111 at-bats in 2000. His rap sheet goes like this:

- Arrested in March of 1984 for reasons still unclear.
- Charged with aggravated assault in 1992 for purposely ramming into his first wife's car.
- Arrested in 1997 for beating his second wife.
- Admitted to taking steroids during his career and estimated that 50 percent of all ballplayers use them.
- Arrested with brother Ozzie in 2001 after a nightclub brawl that left him with 20 stitches and a broken nose.
- Blew off subsequent court date, for which an arrest warrant was issued. (He may still be at large. If you see someone who resembles José, a sure-fire way to identify him is to hit him a fly ball. If the ball hits the guy in the head, that's Canseco!).

THE HEADHUNTER

In 1986, long before he tossed a chunk of splintered bat at Mike Piazza in the 2000 Series and developed a well-deserved reputation for headhunting, Roger Clemens had established his MO: substitute intimidation for dialogue. After Clemens won that year's MVP award, Henry Aaron told the press that he didn't think pitchers should be eligible for it. "I wish he were still playing," said Clemens. "I'd probably crack his head open to show him how valuable I was."

In addition to his homicidal inclinations, the Rocket also double-talked his way out of New York, telling the Yankees he had retired, then un-retiring less than two months later to play with his hometown Houston Astros.

THE BOOMER

1975: The sister of young David Wells scrapes his sun-burned back with her fingernails, so he punches her and breaks her jaw.

1997: Wells, now pitching for the Yankees, threatens to punch out George Steinbrenner while arguing with him about the porous Stadium security that had allowed a fan to turn a catchable ball hit off Wells into a home run.

2002: Wells gets belted by a drunken heckler in a Manhattan diner.

This is all you need to know about Boomer, beloved by Yankee fans, who identify with his boorish, vulgar imma-turity, traits all too obvious to major league executives. According to Buster Olney, who covered the Yankees for the *New York Times*: "No fewer than seven teams released, traded, or allowed Wells to depart as a free agent, mainly because of conditioning problems, self-centeredness, and his knack for saying the wrong thing at the wrong time."

Boomer's such a free spirit that he apparently didn't read his own autobiography, *Perfect, I'm Not*, and disputed numerous passages, such as his contention that he pitched his perfect game while half drunk.

Finally, just one day after Wells bragged to reporters about his lack of conditioning, he suffered a pre-game "freak" back injury that forced him to leave Game 5 of the World Series after just one inning. (The Marlins battered his replacement, José Contreras, and won the game.)

The Dynasty Reunion

What the members of the Yankee Dynasty will be doing 10 years from now:

✦ **Paul O'Neill:** Leading corporate anger-management seminars.

✦ **Don Zimmer:** Bench coach for Tampa Bay Devil Rays, who are now playing in the International League.

✦ **Chuck Knoblauch:** Demanding to be permitted entrance to Manhattan nightclub Veruka, not realizing that it closed 15 years earlier.

✦ **Joe Torre:** Managing Vatican softball team, which finishes last, behind even the Scientologists.

✦ **Darryl Strawberry:** Selling his autographed kidneys on eBay.

✦ **Andy Pettitte:** Raptured.

✦ **Roger Clemens:** Left behind—for throwing inside at God.

✦ **Luis Sojo:** Host of *Sábado Gigante*.

✦ **Tino Martinez:** Missing "bunt" sign during Old-Timers Game and put on "senior waivers" by . . .

✦ **George Steinbrenner:** Cryogenically frozen; thawed out once a year to fire manager.

Chapter Eleven

YANKEES SUCK
ACROSS AMERICA[1]

The great thing about knowing that the Yankees suck is that it's a universal sentiment—the Esperanto of sports fandom that unites people of all races, creeds, colors, and gender preferences in a bubbling cauldron of hatred. For those of you new to Yankee Hating, and for you veterans who never tire of rubbing salt in your own wounds, here's your guide to how the Yanks suck across America.

BOSTON

Here are 13 reasons why Red Sox Nation is at war with the Yanks: 1938, 1939, 1941, 1942, 1949, 1977, 1978, 1998, 1999, 2000, 2001, 2002, and 2003. Those are the years the Sox were runners-up to New York for the American League pennant.

Even before the Curse of the Bambino, Bucky "F***ing" Dent and Aaron "F***ing II" Boone, Boston fans had a *casus belli* toward the Yankees. In the years before and after they bought Babe Ruth from the Sox, the Yanks also fleeced Boston out of star pitchers Carl Mays, Herb Pennock, and Waite Hoyt. When commissioner Kenesaw Mountain Landis nullified the sale of Mays as being not in the best interests of baseball, Yanks' owner Jacob Ruppert and the Yankees sued him and won. This pattern of betrayal by Sox stars continued in the 1990s, when Wade Boggs and Roger Clemens each jumped ship to the Yanks just in time to cruise home with a ring.

For those of you who have arrived in the Northeast from Alpha Centauri, 1978 is still a bitter memory to Sox fans, thanks to Dent's implausible seventh-inning home run that helped the Yanks knock off Boston in a one-game playoff for the American League East crown at Fenway

Park. This remained the franchise's primal tragedy, their version of Sherman's March—until Aaron Boone assumed Dent's mantle in the 2003 ALCS, when he launched a Tim Wakefield knuckler into the left-field stands and stabbed millions of Sox fans in the heart with his walk-off series-winner.

The open warfare that ensues in the stands at a Yanks–Red Sox tussle is often mirrored on the field. In a 1976 regular-season game at Yankee Stadium, New York's Lou Piniella collided with Boston catcher Carlton Fisk at home plate and came up swinging. In the ensuing fight, Red Sox pitcher Bill Lee was body-slammed and wound up with an injury that he claimed destroyed his career. In the 2003 ALCS, Yanks' outfielder Karim Garcia—after he'd been hit by Pedro Martinez—knocked down Sox second baseman Todd Walker and started a bench-clearing brawl that ended with Martinez matadorially pushing a charging, nostril-flaming Don Zimmer onto the Fenway Park infield. Last year, Alex Rodriguez was baited by Jason Varitek into taking a punch at him, an incident that woke up the slumbering Sox and fueled their late-season surge.

So for 85 years, Sox fans have raged at the marauders

from the Bronx, a hostility that blankets the entire franchise all the way to the online merchandising outlets, which offer "Boston Red Sox Boy and Girl Pee on N.Y. Yankees" decals and magnets—when biting the bobblehead off Derek Jeter dolls isn't enough.

Boston's stunning ALCS win in 2004 may yet prove a mixed blessing. Yes, it lifted one curse, but all those years of obsessing about the Yankees has turned many Red Sox fans into mini-Steinbrenners, for whom anything but a world championship is unacceptable. Be careful who you hate, Red Sox Nation, lest you become them.

BALTIMORE

Oriole fans have many valid reasons for the bile, odium, and white-hot rage they harbor toward the Yankees:

1. The Yanks started out as the original Baltimore Orioles, and their move to New York in 1903 left Baltimore without a major league team for a half century. As one Birds fan put it, "It should have been the O's winning all those championships."

2. Mike "Judas" Mussina (as he was called by one fan),

the All-Star pitcher who bailed out for the Bronx after spending his entire career with Baltimore.

3. The guy who launched the Yankees Dynasty never played an inning for the team—Jeffrey Maier, the 12-year-old who stole a run from Tony Tarasco and the Orioles in Game 1 of the 1996 ALCS. Here's what some Baltimore fans had to say about little Jeffrey:

"I want to pistol-whip him."

"Maier is Spawn of Satan!"

"Maier symbolizes the arrogant, stereotypical, 'I can get away with anything' Yankee fan, the Yankee-loving media, and the win-at-all-costs mentality of Steinbrenner. . . . I still wish personal harm on Jeffrey."

TORONTO

Although Canadians are by nature less vituperative than their American counterparts, Blue Jays fans can compile enough reasons to summon up an anti-Yankee snit. For one thing, they've spent most of the last 30 years finishing behind the Yanks, including six straight third-place finishes from 1998 to 2003. (They finished fifth last year, 33½ games behind the Yankees.) Then of course there's the

Winfield Seagull incident. (See Chapter 5: The Dark Side of the Yankees.) And the exchange rate, which is one reason that the Jays are limited to a payroll of $50 million or so, less than one-third that of the Yanks.

TAMPA BAY

Fans of the Tampa Bay Devil Rays must endure so much: In addition to being intra-divisional patsies, they're a virtual colony of the Yankees. In their own home town, the Rays are second-class citizens to the Yanks' spring-training complex and Single A ball team, the Tampa Yankees. And Tampa is the home of George Steinbrenner.

MINNESOTA

Three reasons why Twins fans hate the Yankees:

1. They're a small-market team that can't possibly compete with the plutocratic Bombers.

2. Inconveniently, they're owned by a tightwad billionaire owner, one of the richest men in America, which causes them moral uneasiness only resolved by blaming pinstriped scapegoats.

3. They suffered playoff losses to the Yanks in 2003 and 2004, with a big meltdown in Game 4 of the latter. The Twins and their All-World starter Johan Santana were cruising 5–0 after five innings when manager Ron Gardenhire was suddenly visited by those succubi, Mystique and Aura. He promptly and inexplicably pulled Santana, and the Yanks came back to win in extra innings.

CHICAGO

Chicagoans have a long historical memory of Yankee aggression. Octogenarian fans still remember the Yanks' Murderers' Row trouncing of the Cubs in 1932, a triumph punctuated by Babe Ruth's famous "called shot" home run off Charlie Root. (When asked if the current generation of Cubs' fans hated the Yankees, *Baseball Prospectus* columnist and Cubs fan Will Carroll replied, "I don't think Cubs fans hate anyone. They're too drunk and stupid."[2])

White Sox fans of a certain vintage undoubtedly recall a famous 1950s brawl between the Yanks and Pale Hose triggered when Art Ditmar threw at Larry Doby, a beanball many at the time thought was racially motivated.

CLEVELAND

The Indians were an arch-rival of the Yanks, especially in the post-WWII generation. Cleveland fans still smart over the way in which the Yankees pried Roger Maris away from them. The Indians front office wouldn't trade the slugging outfielder to New York, and instead sent him to Kansas City, who held Maris for a year, then practically gave him away to the Yanks. (See below.)

The Yanks delivered a fresher wound to the city's civic pride when they won the 1998 ALCS from Cleveland, four games to two.

KANSAS CITY

If any fans have a right to despise the New York Yankees, it's those of the Kansas City Athletics, who know just how the Chinese felt toward imperial Japan. Even the team's birth was tainted by Yankee corruption. In 1954, businessman Arnold Johnson, who had already bought Yankee Stadium and a minor league team in K.C. in 1952, bid for the Philadelphia A's. Yankees owner Dan Topping helped Johnson—whose bid was suspected not to be the highest—win the team. In exchange, Johnson willingly allowed New York to treat the K.C. Athletics as a combination farm club and private fief. In six years of trades—and in one of the most shameful and relatively unexplored episodes in baseball history—the Yankees stole the A's best players in exchange for mediocrities.

K.C. gave the Yanks Enos Slaughter, Bobby Shantz, Art Ditmar, Clete Boyer, Ralph Terry, Hector Lopez, and Roger Maris (in one of the most lopsided trades in history, Maris, Kent Hadley, and Joe DeMaestri went to New York for Norm Siebern, Hank Bauer, Marv Throneberry, and Don Larsen.) The Yankees, in fact, rarely even traded players with any other team during this period, in which they won four more pennants in a row beginning in 1955, while the new Kansas City team struggled to stay out of the cellar. Ten members of the 1961 Yankees, considered by many the greatest team of all time, came from the Athletics.

Kansas City's latter-day major-league representative, the Royals, lost playoff series to New York in 1976, 1977, and 1978, before finally beating them in 1981.

DETROIT

As noted baseball scribe Richard Lally put it when asked what Tigers fans hold against the Yankees, he replied, "Detroit won over one hundred games with one of its greatest teams ever. In 1961. 'Nuff said."

ANAHEIM

It was 2003, the Chinese year of the Rally Monkey, the team totem whose appearance on the Angels' scoreboard cast a spell over the hated Yankees in the ALCS. The Halos clubbed the Yanks' pitchers like baby seals en route to a 4–1 series win.

OAKLAND

Anti-Yank sentiment followed the Athletics franchise to its third and current destination, fed by two main currents: (1) In the 1970s, the Yanks signed Catfish Hunter and Reggie Jackson, mainstays of the powerhouse A's of the early 1970s; (2) Painful losses to the Yanks in both the 2001 and 2002 AL Division Series. The former featured Derek Jeter's football-option pass relay to Jorge Posada, which nailed a lumbering, upright Jeremy Giambi at home in the Yanks' 1–0 Game 3 win that kept the Bombers alive and turned the Series around in a New York minute.

TEXAS (ARLINGTON)

It was bad enough that the Yankees beat the Rangers in three straight Division Series (1996, 1998, 1999) by a combined nine games to one. But then Ranger fans saw Alex Rodriguez connive his way out of town in early 2004, in return for whom they got Alfonso Soriano, who: (1) was two years older than his listed age, as Texas found out; (2) had a mediocre year; and (3) will still make too much money in arbitration for the Rangers' modest payroll and will force them to trade him.

Jamey Newburg, creator of the excellent newburgreport.com Rangers website, expressed the inner feelings of Rangers fans toward the Yankees: "The Rangers had never been a playoff team from 1972 until they played the Yanks in 1996, when we won Game 1 in New York, then lost nine straight. We felt like, "We've finally moved out of 25 years of piss-poor baseball, but we couldn't get a series against anybody but the Yankees, who have such a bigger payroll. There was also a sense that the Yankees weren't concerned about us, that they were always looking ahead to Boston or the World Series. They were the big bad villain."

SEATTLE

In 2001, the Mariners broke the American League record for wins with 116 (trumping the 1998 Yankees' 114), but the Yanks doused their pixie dust by thrashing them four games to one in the League Championship Series.

NATIONAL LEAGUE IMPRESSIONS

ARIZONA (PHOENIX)

After the 2001 season, in which the Diamondbacks had finally ended the Yankees Dynasty, their owner, Jerry Colangelo, came to a handshake agreement with David Wells, only to have George the Bully swoop down and sign him away from Arizona. This may have been George's revenge for Colangelo's playing "New York, New York" repeatedly after Arizona blasted the Yankees in Game 6 in Arizona. Colangelo said at the time, "I heard it over and over and over in Yankee Stadium, and if they can't take a little fun, then the hell with them."

WASHINGTON

With a new team in tow, albeit in the National League, the D.C. fans can rekindle a hatred of the Yankees that reached its creative apex with Douglas Wallop's book *The Year the Yankees Lost the Pennant* and its musical adaptation, *Damn Yankees* (in which loyal Senators fan Joe Hardy goes all Faust just to help his team beat the Yanks).

NEW YORK: QUEENS

The Mets came into existence a laughing stock during the waning years of the Yankee dynasty. Many of their fans were residual Dodger and Giant followers, and the memory of so many defeats at the hands of the Yankees was still fresh. In their first three years, they finished last while the Yanks won the pennant and in 1962 the World Series, yet the Mets regularly outdrew their crosstown rivals, posting better attendance numbers in 12 of their first 14 seasons. In fact, it wasn't until the beginning of the last Yankee dynasty that the Yankees finally caught up to the Mets in annual attendance. From the Mets' inception through the strike-shortened 1994 season, more New Yorkers made their way to Flushing than to the Bronx in 21 of 33 seasons.

Of course, that provides little comfort to Mets fans, who watched in horror as Armando Benitez blew the save in Game 1 of the 2000 World Series against the Yanks, on the road to an eventual Series loss. The Mets haven't fared any better in the regular season, having split or lost every series matchup between the two teams since the beginning of interleague play through 2003. While a three-game sweep at Shea in 2004 did manage to clinch the season series and make it safe for New York's National League fan base to wear their team's cap on the subways, it was still only a drop in the bucket. Boston fans may hate their Yankee counterparts, but at least they get to go home to their own; Mets fans have to live with the enemy and bear his noxious presence on a daily basis. How do Mets fan really feel about the Yankees? One fan wrote on a website, "Steinbrenner eats babies."

NEW YORK: MANHATTAN

The New York Giants shared their home on Hilltop Park, called the Polo Grounds, with the fledgling Yankees from 1913 to 1922, at the end of which time the Ruthian Bombers outdrew the Giants and went on to dethrone them as the city's favorite team. Oh, and they also beat them in five straight World Series from 1923 to 1951, and a sixth if you count their win over the San Francisco Giants in 1962.

NEW YORK: BROOKLYN

"Dem Bums," as the Dodgers were known for decades, suffered ignominy while the Yanks were erecting a mythic presence in baseball's Golden Age. To the Dodgers' working-class, immigrant fans, the Yankees were a combination of Hitler and Big Capital. In the 1941 World Series, Dodger catcher Mickey Owens's passed ball on a third strike to Tommy Henrich kept the Yanks alive long enough for them to win the game and the Series. After the war, Dodger fans watched while Casey Stengel, considered a hapless loser when he'd helmed the Dodgers, took over the reins in the Bronx and lead the Yanks to an unequaled championship run that included 1947, 1949, 1951, 1952, 1953, and 1956 World Series wins over the Dodgers.

NOTES

1. This chapter is based on material from baseballlibrary. com, Total Baseball, BaseballProspectus.com, and responses to author's queries through online chat rooms of fan sites.

2. E-mail exchange with the author, 2004.

Firable Offenses

Worst (sub .500) Yankee Regular-Season Performances

Season	W	L	PCT	GB
1992	76	86	.469	20
1991	71	91	.438	20
1990	67	95	.414	21
1989	74	87	.460	14.5
1973	80	82	.494	17
1969	80	81	.497	28.5
1967	72	90	.444	20
1966	70	89	.440	26.5
1965	77	85	.475	25
1925	69	85	.448	28.5
1918	60	63	.488	13.5
1917	71	82	.464	28.5
1915	69	83	.454	32.5
1914	70	84	.455	30
1913	57	94	.377	38
1912	50	102	.329	55
1909	74	77	.490	23.5
1908	51	103	.331	39.5
1907	70	78	.473	21
1905	71	78	.477	21.5
1902	50	88	.362	34

Worth Apologizing Over...

Worst Yankee Postseason Performances Ever

Year	Round	Opponent	Game 1	Game 2	Game 3	Game 4
2004	ALCS	Red Sox	10–7, NYY	3–1, NYY	19–8, NYY	6–4, Bos (12)
2003	WS	Marlins	3–2, Fla	6–1, NYY	6–1, NYY	4–3, Fla (12)
2002	ALDS	Angels	8–5, NYY	8–6, Ana	9–6, Ana	9–5, Ana
2001	WS	Diamondbacks	9–1, Arz	4–0, Arz	2–1, NYY	4–3, NYY (10)
1997	ALDS	Indians	8–6, NYY	7–5, Cle	6–1, NYY	3–2, Cle
1995	ALDS	Mariners	9–6, NYY	7–5, NYY (15)	7–4, Sea	11–8, Sea
1981	WS	Dodgers	5–3, NYY	3–0, NYY	5–4, LA	8–7, LA
1980	ALCS	Royals	7–2, KC	3–2, KC	4–2, KC	X
1976	WS	Reds	5–1, Cin	4–3, Cin	6–2, Cin	7–2, Cin
1964	WS	Cardinals	9–5, StL	8–3, NYY	2–1, NYY	4–3, StL
1963	WS	Dodgers	5–2, LA	4–1, LA	1–0, LA	2–1, LA
1960	WS	Pirates	6–5, Pit	16–3, NYY	10–0, NYY	3–2, Pit
1957	WS	Braves (Milwaukee)	3–1, NYY	4–2, Mil	12–3, NYY	7–5, Mil (10)
1955	WS	Dodgers (Brooklyn)	6–5, NYY	4–2, NYY	8–3, Bklyn	8–5, Bklyn
1942	WS	Cardinals	7–4, NYY	4–3, StL	2–0, StL	9–6, StL
1926	WS	Cardinals	2–1, NYY	6–2, StL	4–0, StL	10–5, NYY
1922	WS	Giants (NY)	3–2, NYG	3–3, TIE	3–0, NYG	4–3, NYG
1921	WS	Giants (NY)	3–0, NYY	3–0, NYY	13–5, NYG	4–2, NYG

Game 5	Game 6	Game 7	Game 8	Result	Team Avg.
5–4, Bos (14)	4–2, Bos	10–3, Bos*	X	Bos–4 NYY –3	.293
6–4, Fla	2–0, Fla	X	X	Fla–4 NYY–2	.261
X	X	X	X	Ana–3 NYY–1	.281
3–2, NYY (12)	15–2, Arz	3–2, Arz	X	Arz–4 NYY–3	.183
4–3, Cle	X	X	X	Cle–3 NYY–2	.259
6–5, Sea (11)**	X	X	X	Sea–3 NYY–2	.259
2–1, LA	9–2, LA	X	X	LA–4 NYY–2	.238
X	X	X	X	KC–3 NYY–0	.255
X	X	X	X	Cin–4 NYY–0	.222
5–2, StL (10)	8–3, NYY	7–5, StL	X	StL–4 NYY–3	.251
X	X	X	X	LA–4 NYY–0	.171
5–2, Pit	12–0, NYY	10–9, Pit	X	Pit–4 NYY–3	.338
1–0, Mil	3–2, NYY	5–0, Mil	X	Mil–4 NYY–3	.248
5–3, Bklyn	5–1, NYY	2–0, Bklyn	X	Bklyn–4 NYY–3	.248
4–2, StL	X	X	X	StL–4 NYY–1	.247
3–2, NYY	10–2, StL	3–2, StL	X	StL–4 NYY–3	.242
5–3, NYG	X	X	X	NYG–4 NYY–0	.203
3–1, NYY	8–5, NYG	2–1, NYG	1–0, NYG	NYG–5 NYY–3	.207

* Thus concluding one of the greatest chokes in the history of professional sports. This back door sweep proved to be a collaps of unprecedented proportions, as it marks the only time a Major League baseball team has given up a 3–0 lead to lose a best-of-seven series.
** For the record, also a back-door sweep.